When You Are Angry with God

by
Pat McCloskey, O.F.M.

PAULIST PRESS
New York/Mahwah

NIHIL OBSTAT: Rev. Hilarion Kistner, O.F.M.
                 Rev. John J. Jennings

IMPRIMI POTEST: Rev. Jeremy Harrington, O.F.M.
                 Provincial
                 October 14, 1986

IMPRIMATUR: ✝ James H. Garland, V. G.
                 Archdiocese of Cincinnati

Excerpt(s) from THE JERUSALEM BIBLE, copyright © 1966 by Darton, Longman & Todd, Ltd. and Doubleday & Company, Inc. Reprinted by permission of the publisher.

Library of Congress Cataloging-in-Publication Data

McCloskey, Patrick.
    When you are angry with God.

    1. Anger—Religious aspects—Christianity.
I. Title.
BV4627.A5M33   1987   248.8'6   87-2261
ISBN 0-8091-2869-1 (pbk.)

Published by Paulist Press
997 Macarthur Boulevard
Mahwah, New Jersey 07430

Printed and bound in the United States of America

Contents

Introduction

In a sense, my urge to write this book began with a visit to a funeral home. A former student, a brilliant young man with a bright future in graduate studies, had fallen asleep at the wheel and had been killed in a one-car crash. Former high school classmates and friends stood in small groups around the funeral parlor, speaking in subdued voices, shocked at the death of someone their age. The mother of the deceased student talked freely of his accomplishments and the senselessness of his death. At one point she said it would take her some time "to talk this over with God." She was neither bitter nor resigned; she was quietly angry and felt that God certainly had some explaining to do. She was prepared to ask God some very hard questions.

But not everyone is ready to ask God those hard questions because admitting anger at God can be very difficult, especially for people who think of themselves as religious. For some men and women, the idea of being angry with God makes as much sense as square circles—the words go together easily but the ideas do not.

Solution? Deny the anger. Since "nice" people never get angry at God and since I want to be "nice" (respectable, able to handle whatever situation arises), therefore I cannot be angry at God. "Nice" men and women can no more be angry at God than "nice" five-year-olds can be angry at their parents. Our experience, however, clearly tells us that five-year-olds who want to be "nice" are sometimes angry at their parents. Children who deny such anger for fear of losing a parent's love will eventually vent their anger on someone or something, usually quite unconnected to their anger. Since it seems that many adults want to be "nice" before God in this sense, they tightly control their feelings and thus simply deny the real cause of their anger. Their anger, however, does not disappear but rather is directed toward innocent bystanders—like us.

In my experience as a counselor and even more as a confessor, I have met people heavily burdened by anger at God, or, more precisely, by anger at what they interpreted as "God's will." And yet often these good people have been reluctant to name that anger and deal with it directly. Whenever they could, they almost always experienced a tremendous sense of relief.

How often do we think that feelings of anger can have only one possible result: destruction? Thus we often think that admitting anger will inevitably lead us to actions which will only make the situation worse. Not many men and women easily come to the conclusion that although they cannot control how they feel, they have many choices about how they will act on those feelings. Admitting anger at God need not lead to agnosticism or atheism; indeed, denying such anger commonly lays the groundwork for a lifeless belief in God.

This is a very personal book—not because I will use many examples of my anger at God (though several will be cited), but because I hope this book will encourage you to deal with feelings which you may have previously denied because you were afraid what might happen if you acknowledged those feelings. Perhaps you have feared that such an admission would result in a "loss of faith." Indeed, admitting your anger may be a necessary step to growing in faith.

If you consider your feelings a Pandora's box best left unopened, then this book is probably not for you. On the other hand, if you suspect that your unacknowledged feelings of anger at God are manipulating you mercilessly, then this book may help you achieve greater peace of mind, grow in faith and become more compassionate toward women, men and children dealing with their own pain and anger.

Sometimes we read books to gain information; at other times a book simply puts into better perspective what we may already know in our guts even if we can't put it into words. This book will offer some new information, but more than that I hope it can be a companion, a support as you venture forth and ask questions whose answers might turn your world upside down (or rightside up)! The old answers may never again be as satisfying.

Perhaps some of those old answers merely covered the pain without really addressing it. Unsatisfactory and debilitating answers can spur us on to seek more adequate and energizing answers. Thus this book should be read with personal investment or not at all. A reader who is simply waiting for *the* answer to human suffering will surely be disappointed. I hope this book will raise and frame the most basic questions about innocent human suffering and anger at God; it can serve as a jumping-off point and as a companion, but not as an answer to make the personal journey unnecessary.

Because this book is intended to help individuals sort out and deal with their feelings about innocent human suffering and anger at God, at the end of each chapter I have included questions to aid private prayer, reflection or journal keeping. Because some groups may find discussing this book helpful, readers will also find opening questions for such discussions. Finally, each chapter will end with suggestions of popular level books and tapes which may help the reader probe that chapter's subject more fully.

The writer Flannery O'Connor once said of an acquaintance who committed suicide, "His tragedy was, I suppose, that he didn't know what to do with his suffering." Do we? I hope this book can help you find more constructive ways of thinking about and dealing with innocent human suffering (the root cause of most anger at God) and thus draw closer to the God who created us in the divine image and placed us in a wonderful but often exasperating world.

1

"Life Isn't Fair"

Life is often frustrating and unfair. A couple may work for forty years and then be swindled out of their life savings in an afternoon. As you read this page, children are being born with syphilis or an addiction to heroin. Chance puts people near terrorist car bombs.

Every day innocent victims are caught in the crossfire of war, racial hatred and family violence. Floods, forest fires and hurricanes simply compound the massive human suffering brought to our attention by radio, TV and the printed word. Each day the morning paper and the TV newscasts present several stories and pictures we would rather forget. *Time*'s cover picture of a child starving in Ethiopia may indicate a story I should read, but I may wish the picture weren't so haunting.

Suffering frustrates us, and very often we don't know what to do with that frustration. How many news stories about a hostage-taking incident end with something like "The man had recently lost his job and family"? Frustrated people sometimes die inside; all too often we notice that only when the person's frustration turns to violence.

Frustrated men and women often seek relief by blaming "the system"—that maze of institutions and rules which seems to restrict people's freedom without offering the support they need when they encounter a tragedy beyond their ability to contain. For example, corporation and bank officials are frequently targets of people's frustrations—in the United States and abroad. "That utility company cares only about profits; this hospital is only out for money; the teachers and administrators in that school don't really care about the students." Increasingly U.S. diplomats and tourists find themselves the lightning rods of local grievances in other countries. People can nurse a loss for months and years by supposing that somewhere somebody had the ability to prevent this tragedy yet refused. If you have ever been on the receiving end of such a complaint against "the system," you know the frustration involved.

Faced with evidence of widespread human suffering, we tend to become numb, to distance ourselves physically ("That's not a problem in my neighborhood") or psychologically ("It's tragic, but what can anybody do about it?"). Men and women unable to distance themselves from suffering more readily accept superficial answers. Neo-Nazi groups in the United States, for example, have drawn more support from farmers on the edge of bankruptcy than from farmers employed by prosperous agribusinesses. An exaggerated nationalism takes an eagle-eyed view of troubles abroad ("What else could you expect there?") but remains blind to problems at home ("Sensationalism, blown out of proportion"). Newspapers, magazines and fringe political parties thriving on conspiracy theories—the ever-present "they"—all have their appeal.

For Jews and Christians, perhaps the most dangerous and superficial answer to human suffering (usually someone else's) is identifying it as "God's will." How can religiously-minded people oppose what they suspect God wills? How easily believers can recommend patience under the most painful circumstances!

Facing Up to Our Anger

It's no wonder that we frequently become angry in the face of today's massive suffering and complex social injustices. Unfortunately, we have a hard time seeing anger as constructive, as something that could precede positive changes. Unlike the TV newscaster in the film *Network* who urged his listeners to raise their windows and shout, "I'm mad as hell, and I'm not going to take this anymore," we tend to say, "That's life; there's nothing you can do about it." Our anger can never become constructive until it is acknowledged.

Since many of us want to be "nice" (respectable, under control), we often deny our anger or find a weaker target for it. Angry with someone at work, I may choose to vent that anger on the driver who cuts in front of me on the expressway. Or I can displace that anger onto friends and family members by fault finding. While they are wondering what's wrong with me today, my anger can hide behind an inhuman perfectionism or deep disappointment that someone else has not come up to my standards.

Denying my anger offers the short-term goal of respectability but the long-term loss of personal integrity. If I say "I'm not angry" when in fact I am, I attempt to live a lie, a very costly and time-consuming tactic which monopolizes my energy and seldom deceives my friends, relatives or work associates. If a husband says he is angry at his next-door neighbor, for example, when he is really angry at his wife, that dishonesty poisons all his relationships inside and outside the family.

Although admitting anger at God can be especially difficult, denying that anger can be even more costly. Generally honest men and women can become very dishonest when it comes to naming and dealing with their anger at God. Only in the face of their own death do some people come to terms with an anger successfully disguised earlier in life.

The Need for Honesty

When Elisabeth Kübler-Ross' *On Death and Dying* was published in 1969, few people suspected how quickly and profoundly that book would influence doctors, nurses, chaplains and the families of the dying. The book rapidly became a best-seller because it helped readers deal with the greatest of human losses (death) as well as understand the grieving process involved in smaller but anticipated losses (e.g., progressive blindness, mastectomy). Many medical schools, nursing programs and seminaries made *On Death and Dying* required reading.

Drawing on interviews with terminally ill patients willing to talk about their illness, Kübler-Ross outlines five stages in the grieving process: denial, anger, bargaining, depression and acceptance. Most dying patients know they are dying even if no one tells them directly. Frequently such patients want to talk about their condition and their feelings but are almost forced into silence by family members, doctors, nurses or chaplains unwilling to deal with the situation and preferring to hold out an unrealistic hope for a new surgical technique, a new drug or some new therapy.

According to Kübler-Ross, patients able to talk about what is happening to them usually move from denial (e.g., "It's just my winter cold") to anger ("Why me, God?" or "The doctors here are all incompetent"). Anger gives way to bargaining for time ("If I can just make it until Ted's graduation or Sue's wedding").

Depression, the fourth stage, is either reactive or preparatory. Reactive depression usually ends when some lingering personal or family question (care of young children, provision for a surviving partner, reconciliation with an estranged friend) is resolved. The person in preparatory depression, on the other hand, is starting to mourn, to withdraw from what has previously made life enjoyable. The final stage of acceptance leaves the person almost void of feelings and waiting for death.

Friends and family members go through the same stages of preparatory grief, but usually not as quickly as the dying person. Indeed, the patient's movement through the grieving process is frequently hindered by someone else's refusal to face the terminal illness. Kübler-Ross cites the case of a woman at the stage of depression whose husband was still denying her imminent death. When he authorized a surgery she had refused, she exploded in anger. Both husband and wife experienced a tremendous freedom when the husband gave up his denial, and they could communicate heart to heart.

For various reasons, not every patient dies in the stage of acceptance. Some terminally ill people die in anger and others while still bargaining for time. Honesty with oneself allows the person to move from one stage to the other; such honesty can be uncomfortable for the patient and for others if the patient begins to express anger at God and the others respond by criticizing the dying person for ingratitude or lack of faith. But terminally ill men and women who are perceptive and honest with themselves, who are cared for by people with whom they can express their feelings and whose friends and family can put patient needs

ahead of their own—such terminally ill women and men
have a good chance of reaching acceptance.

Kübler-Ross' book has helped to show that statements
such as "Cheer up, stop talking like that" or "You
shouldn't feel that way" always reflect the speaker's need,
not that of the suffering person. Often medical personnel,
chaplains and family members have missed valuable opportunities to help the suffering or have actually made the
suffering worse because they did not realize or would not
admit their own anger at God or fear of dying. If they can
become more honest with themselves, they can offer
greater help to the dying person.

Kübler-Ross' book has helped people in preparatory
grief realize that they need to be honest about their feelings. That same often difficult honesty is needed wherever
women, men and children are confronted by innocent human suffering.

A Difficult Honesty

Men and women angry at God sometimes shock others
who respond with a theological answer justifying God.
What the angry person needs, however, is the freedom to
express that anger verbally. When I am angry at God—for
whatever reason—the worst thing I can do is to deny that
feeling or allow someone else to shame me into silence.
Frightening as it may be to face that anger, anything less is
as futile as spitting against the wind. Just as dying patients
experience a tremendous sense of relief when they see that
friends or family members are able to hear honest talk
about the present and future, so the angry person who can
stop pretending he/she is *not* angry experiences a tremendous sense of relief. Without any facade to maintain, everyone becomes more free. How we handle grief and anger—

our own and others—determines in large part our inner growth or stagnation. Unfortunately, according to the popular wisdom the mere passing of time brings healing for the grieving.

A Tricky Proverb

At St. Bonaventure University in Olean, New York, there is a freestanding clock inscribed with four Latin sayings about time. For all the times I passed that clock during summer school, the proverb I remember best is "Tempus sanat vulnera" (Time heals wounds). If only life were that simple! Like most proverbs, this one contains an element of truth, but taken at face value it is false. How many times have you heard someone say that the suffering person "will get over it"? And how often do people "get over it" only by telling themselves lies?

Time can help heal a wound but only after something more important has been done first. A medical analogy may help here. If I break my arm and someone sets it improperly, time will make permanent what was only temporarily crooked. I believe that fractures of the human heart follow a similar pattern.

With time we may find a better answer to some suffering rather than permanently accept the first explanation which suggests itself. If, for example, I suffer a serious injury and then immediately conclude that God is punishing me for some evil I have done, time will not heal that moral-psychological wound. Time can only dull the pain; my wound can never heal properly until I go back and reconsider my first explanation for why this suffering occurred. If that first answer is like the broken bone improperly set, time will not cure the situation. Just as doctors sometimes have to break a bone in order to set it properly, so we often have to reconfront our initial loss if the wound is ever to heal properly. Friends, family members, professional counselors or members of the clergy can help us face that initial loss and deal with it more adequately.

One such personal story can illustrate many others. A high school student whose younger brother had been partially paralyzed as a result of a freak accident became rather bitter and disinterested in life. One day as we talked about his brother's accident and what part God did or did not play in it, I saw this student starting to face his anger at God and deal with it more adequately. Later events suggested that the student (now graduated) had made peace with God on this issue. Almost the worst thing I could have said to that student when he started to admit his anger at God would be "You shouldn't feel like that" or agree that his brother's suffering was "God's will" (without any qualifications).

Is It Really God's Will?

Why didn't God step in and prevent the accident which forever changed the life of this student's brother? Why doesn't God protect the swindled elderly couple, the baby born with syphilis or the children starving in Ethiopia? If God can count the hairs on a person's head and generously feed the birds as the Gospel says he does (Mt 6:26), then why doesn't he come through when you really need him?

One answer to that question makes a distinction between the *active* will of God (e.g., that all people be saved and enjoy the fullness of life with God) and the *permissive* will of God (e.g., God does not favor forest fires or murder but he has made a world in which both are possible). When people speak of some tragedy as God's will, they usually mean his *permissive* will rather than a careful choice by God to inflict some suffering on an individual or group. But unfortunately what one person intends to say is not always what another person hears; thus God can seem very cruel.

Does anybody have a better answer? In 1981, Rabbi Harold Kushner's highly personal book *When Bad Things Happen to Good People* touched a raw nerve in the American psyche; almost immediately readers drove this book to the top of the non-fiction best-seller list. Kushner's book reveals his own crisis of faith in dealing with his son Aaron's progeria, that rare and always fatal disease which ages a person prematurely. Progeria claimed Aaron's life two days after his fourteenth birthday. In the ten years between the diagnosis and Aaron's death, this anguished father and rabbi sought to make some sense of the tragedy. What he quickly found, however, were books and people more concerned with defending God's honor in such matters than with comforting a grieving family. During this personal odyssey, Rabbi Kushner began to reconsider the comfort he had been offering to grieving members of his congregation.

It's easy to hope that suffering will at least ennoble the person, make that individual more thoughtful or compassionate. But that explanation of suffering is riddled with problems and tends to make sense only to someone rather unaffected by suffering. To men and women in a search like Rabbi Kushner's, that explanation of suffering sounds very hollow and heartless.

Don't we suspect that the "suffering-can-ennoble-a-person" idea is really a fraud, a convenient excuse not to face the situation honestly, an attempt to let God off the hook too easily? True, some people seem to grow in wisdom and character after some tragedy, but our experience also tells us that many suffering men and women become extremely bitter. Some commit suicide; others rethink their ideas on euthanasia. I believe most of us have seen many suffering women and men become old before their time. As their horizons shrink, they shrivel up inside and die spiritually long before they draw their last breath.

Because we are so uncomfortable with suffering, we sometimes avoid visiting a friend or relative in the hospital or nursing home. Visiting a child recovering from an appendectomy is much easier than visiting someone who has suffered a stroke. Going to the funeral home can also be very painful. At times we fear saying the wrong thing, and yet deep down we wonder if there is, in fact, any "right" thing to say. "I'm very sorry" seems inadequate. What *is* God's will in all of this?

Even if we have lost an aged friend or relative and someone assures us, "It's a blessing," we may be tempted to scream back, "No it isn't." If someone tells us that God never sends a cross without the grace to bear it, we may be more tempted to commit murder than at any other time in life. The glib phrase "It's God's will" has probably produced more atheists and dispirited believers than any other phrase in our vocabulary!

Rabbi Kushner's book summarizes his search for the meaning of his son's terminal illness: which answers made sense and which ones seemed to offer help but didn't. Certainly the rabbi did not have the same understanding of God by the book's end as he did in the beginning. Nor did he find some overarching purpose in human suffering.

What Kushner did discover was his freedom to decide which of many possible meanings this suffering would have for him. Borrowing the phrase from theologian Dorothy Soelle, Kushner speaks of "God's martyrs" (witnesses in favor of God) and "the devil's martyrs" (witnesses against God and the meaningfulness of a moral life). The survivors must decide if the suffering person is a witness for or against God. Chapter 6 of this book will take a closer look at the life beyond this one and Kushner's objections to the idea.

Rabbi Kushner's search brought him to greater peace before God; however, neither he nor any other writer can give a reader that same peace. Some questions *we* have to ask and struggle to answer; no one can do that for us because we become different people along this most personal of journeys. God is not threatened by hard questions though we might be scared to ask them. "Is suffering ever 'God's will'?" tops the list of hard questions.

"Act of God"

Naturally we realize that some suffering is caused by forces of nature which even the best planning cannot prevent. Volcanoes, typhoons and floods are commonly described as "acts of God." Of course, our language here is rather odd. Hurricane Edward is an "act of God" but Niagara Falls isn't. God usually gets blamed for devastating floods but often receives no credit for sunny days. Strange.

Although we can account for much of human suffering through an abuse of human freedom, that will not explain everything. The so-called "acts of God" must bear their share of suffering caused. The evening news reminds us that an entire town can be devastated without warning. Maybe the town will come back stronger than before; maybe not. In one day in May 1985 a tidal wave in Bangladesh killed at least fifteen thousand people. A few months later earthquakes in Mexico and a volcano in Columbia killed another thirty thousand people. If God is good, how can this happen?

We can say that God didn't decide to send this tidal wave and that volcano; they had "natural" causes. But if God created the world, why didn't he prevent such things? Couldn't he have made a world without floods? Couldn't God have made a world without the progeria which killed

Aaron Kushner? Why do we have to learn to live with such things?

What does saying that some disease or natural disaster represents "God's will" accomplish? Usually the innocent victims or friends and relatives feel a double burden: being angry at God because of the initial suffering and then feeling guilty because "nice" people never get angry at God. Another personal example may help to illustrate this difficulty .

My First Real Anger at God

Looking back now, I see that my life was pretty easy until I was a junior in high school. Of course, I had done my share of complaining that "life isn't fair," but nothing really shook my faith in God until two nephews were born several months prematurely and died a few days later.

I was away at school, and I remember my father's letter saying that they had been born, named, and baptized immediately, and that I should pray for their survival. Up to that time I had prayed for various people but never for someone literally in a life-or-death situation. Earlier prayers of petition might have concerned more trivial matters, but this was certainly big league praying. Here was the clearest and most painful case of innocent suffering I had ever encountered. How could God *not* hear my prayers and those of our whole family for those tiny infants? For some reason I felt confident that they would make it, and therefore I was devastated when I learned that my nephews had died.

How could a good God let this happen? To say that my nephews died of "natural causes" seemed heartless and dishonest. Furthermore, their death did not seem like "God's will" no matter from what angle I viewed this tragedy. Nevertheless, at that time I thought that "nice" people never get angry at God. Though puzzled and hurt, they somehow "get over it" and "life goes on." Besides, my religion taught me that baptized infants who die go straight to heaven. Who was I to complain? Slowly life returned to a new kind of normalcy. Two years later my brother and sister-in-law had a healthy baby girl, and I was ready to let God off the hook.

A Bigger Challenge

If when I was a junior in high school I was ready to excuse God for the deaths of two newly-born nephews, when I was twenty-five an even greater challenge arose. Within three weeks my father was discovered to have an inoperable malignant tumor and my mother suffered a massive stroke which hospitalized her for two months. All of this happened just as my father was about to retire from his dental practice and enjoy a Florida condominium he and my mother had recently purchased.

Since my parents were hospitalized in separate cities, at one point that summer I was driving one hundred and twenty miles round trip each day to pick my father up after his chemotherapy, drive back to see my mother (by now in physical therapy) and then take my father back to his hospital. Each day I made that trip, I was by myself for about an hour and a half—long enough to ask God some hard questions. The lives of my older sister and my three older brothers were also turned topsy-turvy. After we had been able to make arrangements for my parents' care at home, life began to be somewhat more normal.

But then came the day I accompanied my father to his office to begin cleaning it out. Forty years of work there were ending like this. He who once seemed so strong was now so weak. And there I was: twenty-five years old, close to an MA in theology, two years away from ordination to the priesthood, and what sense, what meaning could I make of a world that was crumbling around me? It was the saddest day of my life, and anger at God wasn't going to improve my parents' physical condition.

Amid all this confusion, my father's primary concern was much more my mother's condition than his own. Slowly she regained limited mobility and some ability to speak. By the time Dad died six months later, he had come to terms with his cancer and with Mom's stroke. He certainly did not die as one of the "devil's martyrs," to use Dorothy Soelle's expression. And I was a little closer to dealing with my topsy-turvy feelings over this excruciating suffering.

Human Freedom

Much—I believe most—of human suffering can be traced to an abuse of human freedom. The child born with a heroin addiction is certainly innocent, but somebody isn't. The terrorist's victims are innocent, but the terrorist isn't. Blaming God for such tragedies hardly seems fair. If men and women weren't free, these things wouldn't happen, of course. But then neither could people develop the medical skills needed to care for that addicted child or the terrorist's victims.

The Book of Genesis assures its readers that evil entered the world through an abuse of human freedom. In a very real sense, God himself is limited. He could have created a world in which disobeying him was impossible; but that would make us zombies, not women and men created "in God's image" (Gn 1:27). In the second century St. Irenaeus of Lyons said that the glory of God is a person fully alive. Individuals are "fully alive" when they grow in appreciating their God-given freedom and its underlying purpose: the ability to choose life (God) and not death (sin). Could God make us free to love without simultaneously opening up the possibility of hatred? Apparently God prefers a world where men and women make significant decisions rather than a world of insignificant choices and guaranteed obedience.

Freedom is basic. God did not have to create anything. Human beings are not automatically prevented from doing the wrong thing. Every story does not have to end happily.

The suffering caused by an abuse of human freedom struck home in a new way in 1982 when I visited Dachau, the Nazi concentration camp started in 1933 not far from Munich. Somehow I expected the camp to be a small one far away from any population center; I expected to get off the train from Munich and be there.

But Dachau is a city as well as a concentration camp; the bus trip from the train station to the camp takes at least ten minutes. And the camp is very large. The main building has been turned into a museum with photographs, letters and maps chronicling the growth of the concentration camp system. A film with newsclips from that era tells the story. One row of prisoner bunkers has been reconstructed; the cement foundations of the other bunkers give mute but eloquent testimony to the monstrous evil done there against thousands of Jews and many Christians and others who opposed the Nazis. The crematorium at Dachau still stands.

If ever a place could be described as evil, I thought to myself, this is it. The Jewish, Protestant and Catholic chapels at the end of the camp seem to cry out stubbornly that God is still good even if men and women can be so evil, even if human freedom can be so abused as to create an obscenity like Dachau. All the people on the bus going back to the Dachau train station were profoundly affected by what they saw and heard.

Can We Make Any Sense out of Human Suffering?

After the attempt on his life in St. Peter's Square in 1981 and after his subsequent recovery from surgery, Pope John Paul II wrote an apostolic letter on the Christian meaning of suffering (*Salvifici doloris*). He says:

> It is obvious that pain, especially physical pain, is widespread in the animal world. But only the suffering human being knows that he is suffering and wonders why; and he suffers in a humanly speaking still deeper way if he does not find a satisfactory answer. (§9)

For many people who believe in God, there can be no satisfactory answer to human suffering until they confront God's role in it. The next chapter will explore what help the Hebrew Scriptures (Old Testament) can offer toward understanding God's role in human suffering.

For Personal Reflection

1. Do you feel irreligious in saying "I am angry at God"? Could such anger be the awkward beginning of a deeper faith?

2. Have you ever experienced a dying person go through the stages of grief which Kübler-Ross describes? What was the most difficult part of that process for you?

3. Have you ever encouraged a dying person *not* to talk about his/her worsening condition? Why? What was the result?

4. Have any instances of suffering been a turning point in your image of God? In what way?

5. Can you identify someone who has been one of the "devil's martyrs" for you? Someone who was one of God's martyrs?

6. Have you ever prayed for something, believing it was certainly "God's will," only to have the prayer seemingly rejected? How did you react?

For Group Discussion

1. Can you point to any examples of anger as being constructive?
2. Why is it so easy for people to tell others, "You shouldn't feel that way"? What are they really communicating?
3. How often do people "get over" some loss by lying to themselves?
4. Do floods, tidal waves or other "acts of God" challenge your faith in God?
5. Do you think that most human suffering is caused by an abuse of human freedom? Have you ever wished God hadn't made us free?
6. Have you ever encouraged anyone to express his/her anger at God? How did the person feel afterward? How did you feel?

Resources

1. Elisabeth Kübler-Ross, *On Death and Dying* (Macmillan, 1969).

2. Harold Kushner, *When Bad Things Happen to Good People* (Avon, 1983).

3. John Paul II, *Salvifici doloris* (On the Christian Meaning of Suffering), (Daughters of St. Paul, 1984).

2

Innocent Suffering
According to the Hebrew Scriptures

If asked to describe the images of God they remember best from the Hebrew Scriptures, many Christians will speak of power, anger and strictness. And surely there is scriptural foundation for all those attributes. The inspired writers, however, did not confine themselves to those images of God; they used many others also. There is a development of theology in the Old Testament. Moses and Qoheleth worshiped the same God but did not see him in exactly the same terms. Unfortunately, this facet of the Hebrew Scriptures remains almost a well-kept secret—to the detriment of adult faith.

If when you were five years old someone asked you to describe your parents, you would probably answer in terms of strength, love and care for you. If at age thirty-five you were asked the same question, would you simply repeat your earlier answer? Certainly not. Although you might use some of the same words (strength, love, care), they would undoubtedly have a deeper meaning. Now, which description of your parents is the correct one—the one you made at age five or at age thirty-five? Or are they both correct, simply reflections of your changing ability to appreciate your parents?

I believe our understanding of God needs to grow with the Hebrew Scriptures. Unfortunately, many Christians know those Scriptures better from Adam to King David than from David to Jesus. Being better acquainted with the second half of the story, however, may broaden and deepen our appreciation for the God of Israel. If all of Scripture is inspired, doesn't all of it deserve our attention, even the parts which may now be unfamiliar or seem hard to understand? If we grow in our images of God, that automatically affects the way we understand ourselves.

The Pentateuch

The first five books of the Bible, the Pentateuch, have a unique place in God's revelation since they trace his providence from Adam and Eve through the time of Moses. Although the Book of Genesis may seem unsophisticated because it reflects the science of that time, surely no other author has given us a better explanation of sin's origin and why the human heart is so often divided.

In their own way, Adam and Eve are angry that God is God and they are not; thus they do the only thing they believe necessary to close the gap between themselves and God. Their rebellion, however, widens the gap though God's love for them remains constant. When Adam and Eve disobey God, they are told that from then on work will be arduous and childbirth painful. For the final editor of the Book of Genesis, suffering is closely linked to sin.

Indeed, Cain suffers after murdering Abel. The writer of that story, however, does not dwell on Abel's innocent suffering but rather continues the narrative. In the time of Noah, we learn, most people were evil and were therefore annihilated in the flood; all the innocent people were saved in the ark. Later, the builders of the tower of Babel are punished for their rashness. Sodom and Gomorrah perish in their wickedness. At every turn the Book of Genesis presents a humanly messy but a theologically tidy world in which good people triumph and evil men and women receive their just punishment.

There is a close call when Abraham almost sacrifices Isaac, but God intervenes and saves Isaac's life. When Jacob steals Esau's inheritance, the Scriptures do not stop to reflect on this theft but rather continue the story about Jacob. In the entire Book of Genesis, the first case of innocent suffering which receives much attention is the brothers' plot against Joseph, but that story ends happily years later when Joseph saves his relatives from starvation and brings his aged father Jacob to Egypt.

In the Book of Exodus, the innocent suffering of the Hebrews prompts God to send Moses to deliver his people from the pharaoh's rule. The Egyptians suffer ten plagues until the pharaoh allows the Hebrews to leave. The rest of the Book of Exodus details the covenant at Mount Sinai and the forty years of wandering in the desert. Throughout this story evil people suffer and good men and women prosper.

In Leviticus and Numbers, God carefully explains all the laws his people must obey, and the Book of Deuteronomy records five sermons about God's fidelity, reminders given immediately before the Israelites enter the promised land. Moses, however, will not accompany them across the Jordan River because of his earlier doubt in the desert (Num 20:1–12). His sin is punished.

Although scholars have identified four theological traditions inerwoven throughout the Pentateuch, the deuteronomic ("second law") theology gives the clearest focus on human suffering. Roughly this view could be summarized as, "Keep God's commandments; remain his special people and you will prosper"—for example, "Honour your father and your mother, as Yahweh your God has commanded you, so that you may have long life and prosper in the country which Yahweh your God is giving you" (Dt 5:16). If the people abandon the Sinai covenant, they will suffer; *group* prosperity or destruction hangs in the balance.

The deuteronomic theology easily explains the rise and the fall of Israel's kings. David disobeys the covenant but has the good sense to repent; Solomon begins well, eventually worships other gods, fails to repent and his kingdom is divided soon after his death. Deuteronomic theology sees the fall of the northern kingdom (Israel) to the Assyrians in 721 B.C. as God's punishment. Likewise, the Babylonian capture of Jerusalem and the razing of Solomon's temple in 587 B.C. represent God's clear judgment against his people.

The loss of political independence and the destruction of their religious focal point (temple worship in Jerusalem) force a national examination of conscience which concludes that the Jewish people are indeed being punished for not being more faithful to the covenant their ancestors made at Mount Sinai. Even when the Jews are allowed to leave Babylon fifty years later and start rebuilding the temple in Jerusalem, they begin to heed the prophets' warnings to strive for personal holiness as well as acceptable sacrifices. In the last five hundred years before Christ's birth, Jewish identity is linked not so much to temple worship as to observing the law of Moses, most especially the rules about ritual cleanliness, circumcision and the sabbath observance.

Deuteronomic theology sees suffering in large terms: Why does the nation suffer? Any attention to suffering on the individual level follows a clear sin/punishment sequence (e.g., David commits adultery with Bathsheba and the child thus conceived dies, 2 Sam 11–12). Under good kings Israel prospers but evil rulers bring disaster on the whole nation.

God as Fearsome and Angry

According to one popular but dangerously oversimplified understanding of the Bible, the Hebrew Scriptures reveal a harsh and angry God while the New Testament presents a merciful and loving God. Already in the second century A.D., the Roman priest Marcion vigorously advanced this idea which was soon declared heretical (ignoring a key part of God's revelation). The Church affirmed that the same God is the author and subject of both Testaments.

While fully accepting the Church's judgment about Marcion's key idea, we can say without any fear of heresy that the Bible gives ample evidence of a people's growth in understanding God. Two very short word counts will roughly illustrate that growth.

According to the *Nelson Concordance to the New American Bible* (the version most U.S. Catholics hear read in church), the word "anger" is used:

240 times in the Bible:
224 times in the Hebrew Scriptures and
  16 times in the New Testament.

According to my count, anger is directly attributed to God 169 times in the Hebrew Scriptures and four times in the New Testament. Fourteen of the 17 times "angered" is used in the Hebrew Scriptures, it is applied to God. The words "wrath" and "fury" are associated with God more often in the Hebrew Scriptures than in the New Testament. Ten times the Old Testament reminds us that God is "slow to anger." The word "fear" is used:

454 times in the Bible:
377 times in the Hebrew Scriptures and
 77 times in the New Testament—

and is respectively applied to God 180 and 16 times. The expression "God-fearing" appears eleven times in the whole Bible, nine of them in the Hebrew Scriptures.

Does all of this prove that Marcion was right? Not at all. Understandably, the biblical writers had no hesitation about using images of fear and anger to emphasize the strength and the uniqueness of Israel's God; after all, these people were constantly tempted to reduce the God of Abraham, Isaac and Jacob, the God of the Mount Sinai covenant, to the level of their pagan neighbors' gods. Belief in one God took hold slowly.

The people's understanding of God grows throughout the Hebrew Scriptures; the development is often painful and zigzagged but ultimately is unmistakable. In the last section of the Hebrew Scriptures to be written, God himself frequently uses the expression "Fear not." Tender and enduring images of God greet the reader of Psalm 136 ("His faithful love endures for ever"), Hosea ("I [God] myself taught Ephraim [Israel] to walk. I myself took them by the arm but they did not know I was the one caring for them") or Job ("The cries of the weak rise to God")—to name a few such passages.

As the people's understanding of God changes, so does their understanding of themselves as God's people. Both changes of viewpoint can be painful but rewarding.

The Psalms:
Confident Assurance of God's Justice

Cries of anguish over personal/national suffering and shouts of gladness over God's steadfast providence fill the psalms, one hundred and fifty songs traditionally ascribed to King David. Almost certainly he composed some of them, but the majority were written approximately between 1000 and 500 B.C. Thus they reflect multiple authors and varied images of God. In general, however, the psalms support the deuteronomic idea that God rewards those who live according to the Mosaic covenant and punishes those who reject that covenant. Even so, some of the psalmists hint that evildoers may not be sufficiently punished and in good time.

Before surveying the psalms for what they tell us about innocent human suffering, we should remember that the psalmists do not presume "heaven" and "hell" in the traditional Christian understanding of those terms. For hundreds of years the Jews believed that those who die, good or evil, go to the same shadowy existence in Sheol. Indeed, Psalm 6 says, "In death there is no remembrance of you; who could sing your praises in Sheol?" (v. 5). Among the Jewish people a strong belief in the afterlife begins only in the third century B.C. (see Chapter 6).

The psalm numbering used in this chapter is the original Hebrew numbering (used in the *New Jerusalem Bible,* the *New American Bible* and in most recent translations); older Catholic translations are one number lower between Psalms 10 and 148.

Psalm 1 presents a theme found throughout the psalter. The just person wants to see God's justice manifested in the world; the wicked do not have a chance. Virtuous men and women will prosper; godless people will vanish. Indeed, "Yahweh watches over the path of the upright, but the path of the wicked is doomed" (v. 6).

In a later psalm the speaker prays that the intrigues of the wicked will cause their downfall (5:10), and elsewhere we learn that God has "ensnared the wicked in the work of their own hands" (9:16). Often evildoers fall into the snares which they have made (7:15 and 57:6); that line expresses very succinctly the fondest hopes of deuteronomic theology. Psalm 10 urges God to rise up and punish the wicked who enjoy a false security; indeed, honest men and women will always see God's face (Ps 11).

A confident psalmist says, "Calling to you, none shall ever be put to shame, but shame is theirs who groundlessly break faith" (25:3). Again, "Countless troubles are in store for the wicked, but one who trusts in Yahweh is enfolded in his faithful love" (32:10). Perseverance is rewarded.

Psalm 37 reflects at length on the fate of sinners and the reward of the just. Evildoers may seem to thrive, but like grass they will quickly wither (v. 1). The psalmist should wait for the Lord and not "get heated over someone who is making a fortune, succeeding by devious means" (v. 7), for the wicked will vanish like smoke (v. 20). "Now I am old, but ever since my youth I never saw an upright person abandoned, or the descendants of the upright forced to beg their bread" (v. 25). The Lord will promote the just to ownership of the land (v. 34). "Observe the innocent, consider the honest, for the man of peace will not lack children" (v. 37).

In Psalm 51, King David prays that God will cleanse him of his sin. According to one rabbinic tradition, David composed this psalm after the prophet Nathan condemned David's adultery with Bathsheba (2 Sam 12:1–12). According to the psalmist, a contrite heart is the only sacrifice which God accepts (v. 17).

Although the psalms very strongly affirm God's justice
and his watchful care for those who follow his ways, the
idea of innocent suffering runs throughout the psalms:

> Why do you take pride in being wicked,
>   you champion in villainy? . . .
> You prefer evil to good,
>   lying to uprightness . . .
> That is why God will crush you,
>   destroy you once and for all,
>   snatch you from your tent,
> uproot you from the land of the living. (52: 1,3,5)

> May their wickedness recoil on those who lie in wait for
>   me.
>   Yahweh, in your constancy destroy them. (54:5)

> Unload your burden onto Yahweh
>   and he will sustain you;
> never will he allow
>   the upright to stumble. (55:22)

> The upright will rejoice to see vengeance done,
>   and will bathe his feet in the blood of the wicked.
> 'So', people will say, 'The upright does have a reward;
>   there is a God to dispense justice on earth.' (58:10–11)

> Once God has spoken,
>   twice have I heard this:
> Strength belongs to God,
>   to you, Lord, faithful love;
>   and you repay everyone as their deeds deserve. (62:11–
>   12)

Psalms 64, 69, 94 and 142 all ask God to punish the wicked.
In Psalm 71 we find an elderly psalmist calling on God's

help as the evildoers close in. Psalm 73 gleefully recounts the false happiness of the wicked and affirms the wisdom of God's ways. Psalm 75 presents God as the just judge of the afflicted. Other psalmists cry out:

> You disperse them [God's enemies] like smoke;
>   as wax melts in the presence of a fire,
>   so the wicked melt at the presence of God. (68:2)

> How much longer, God, will the enemy blaspheme?
>   Is the enemy to insult your name for ever? (74:10)

> Does God forget to show mercy?
>   In anger does he shut off his tenderness?
> And I said, 'This is what wounds me,
>   the right hand of the Most High has lost its strength.'
>   (77:9–10)

As if to answer the insistent questions of all these psalmists, God responds:

> If only my people would listen to me,
>   if only Israel would walk in my ways,
> at one stroke I would subdue their enemies,
>   turn my hand against their opponents. (81:13–14)

Psalm 86 asks for a proof of God's favor, a sign to silence the psalmist's enemies (v. 17). The author of Psalm 88 feels God's wrath and asks: "Why, Yahweh, do you rebuff me, turn your face away from me? . . . You have deprived me of friends and companions, and all that I know is the dark" (vv. 14, 18). The anguished speaker of Psalm 102 concludes that God abides forever and the wicked do not; Psalm 109 recounts the suffering caused by friends who have become enemies. The final psalmist who reflects on innocent suffering cries out:

> Do not let my attackers prevail,
>> but let them be overwhelmed by their own malice.
> May red-hot embers rain down on them,
>> may they be flung into the mire once and for all.
> May the slanderer find no rest anywhere,
>> may evil hunt down violent men implacably.
> I know that Yahweh will give judgement for the wretched,
>> justice for the needy.
> The upright shall praise your name,
>> the honest dwell in your presence. (140:9–13)

The authors of the psalms are certainly well acquainted with innocent human suffering, but they do not believe that God is to be blamed for such suffering. In time he will vindicate his faithful people and establish his justice. The confidence found in the psalms, however, does not keep other biblical writers from asking God some hard questions.

Is This Any Way to Treat Your People?

God's ways are openly questioned in the Book of Habakkuk, probably written at the time of profound national crisis, between the battle of Carchemish (605 B.C.) and the destruction of Jerusalem (587 B.C.). At Carchemish, the Egyptians, then protectors of Judah, had been decisively beaten by the Babylonians, the emerging superpower. Thus Babylon is poised to capture Jerusalem and destroy the kingdom of Judah. Shortly before this decisive battle, Judah's saintly King Josiah had died; perhaps he was assassinated. Thus the people began to reconsider their ideas about God's providence. Since Josiah had been a zealous promoter of deuteronomic theology, the people wondered, "How can God do this to his people?" Habakkuk ponders his people's future and questions God.

> Then Yahweh answered me and said,
> 'Write the vision down,
> inscribe it on tablets
> to be easily read.
> For the vision is for its appointed time,
> it hastens towards its end and it will not lie;
> although it may take some time, wait for it,
> for come it certainly will before too long.
> You see, anyone whose heart is not upright will succumb,
> but the upright will live through faithfulness.' (2:2–4)

God is preparing the final victory of justice—even if Babylon conquers Jerusalem. This book ends with Habakkuk's new and more mature praise of God's saving action for his people:

> (For the fig tree is not to blossom,
> nor will the vines bear fruit,
> the olive crop will disappoint
> and the field will yield no food;
> the sheep will vanish from the fold;
> no cattle in the stalls.)
> But I shall rejoice in Yahweh,
> I shall exult in God my Saviour.
>
> Yahweh my Lord is my strength,
> he will make my feet as light as a doe's,
> and set my steps on the heights. (3:17–19)

The problem of innocent suffering remains, but God has vindicated his goodness. The next biblical writer, however, is not so easily satisfied.

Job: Probing the Limits
of Deuteronomic Theology

The writer of the Book of Job (c. 600–450 B.C.) is fully aware of the "keep-God's-law-and-everything-will-be-fine" theology, but the writer is unconvinced that this theology adequately deals with all human suffering. Thus we are introduced to a pious, rich man and his seven sons and three daughters. Job's good fortune leads Satan to taunt God with the suggestion that Job's piety will quickly disappear if he loses his children and his possessions. God allows Satan this power; Job's children are killed and his livestock is destroyed, and yet Job does not curse God. Satan comes back into God's presence, refusing to admit defeat. God then allows Satan to send a dreadful disease on Job. Even then, Job, afflicted with "malignant ulcers from the sole of his foot to the top of his head" (2:7), will not curse God.

At this point Satan fades out of the story and is replaced by three friends who come to comfort Job. These friends, unfortunately, expend more energy defending their idea of God's justice than comforting Job. Surely, they reason, all Job's troubles will disappear if he will simply acknowledge that his sins have caused all this suffering.

Job vigorously rejects their "solution," at one point crying out:

> Whatever you know, I know too;
>   I am in no way inferior to you.
> But my words are intended for Shaddai;
>   I mean to remonstrate with God.
> As for you, you are only charlatans,
>   All worthless as doctors! (13:2–4)

Job protests his innocence; God is not punishing him. Nor does Job believe in an afterlife though he is confident that eventually he will be vindicated (19:25). Against the smug theology of his friends, Job says that the world is not so simple. Why do the wicked prosper so often?

When God finally intervenes to break this theological deadlock, he does not answer Job's complaints except to say that Job cannot question God as an equal since Job did not create the world as God did. Throughout chapters 38–41, God puts Job on the defensive with questions such as:

> Where were you when I laid the earth's foundations?
> Tell me, since you are so well-informed!
> Who decided its dimensions, do you know?
> Or who stretched the measuring line across it? (38:4–5)

or

> Do you know when mountain goats give birth?
> Have you ever watched deer in labour?
> Have you ever counted the months that they carry their
>   young?
> Do you know when they give birth? (39:1–2)

God continues his "answer" by contrasting Job's puny strength to that of Behemoth (the hippopotamus) and Leviathan (the crocodile) [40:15–41:26].

Finally Job capitulates, saying: "You have told me about great works that I cannot understand, about marvels which are beyond me, of which I know nothing. . . . Before, I knew you only by hearsay but now, having seen you with my own eyes, I retract what I have said, and repent in dust and ashes" (42:3b, 5–6). In this book's epilogue God angrily criticizes Job's three friends for their cruel comfort—in effect, for their at-all-costs deuteronomic theology. As the story closes, God restores Job's wealth, giving him another seven sons and three daughters.

The Book of Job represents a major breakthrough in the theology of innocent suffering. Job's anger with God is not shamed into silence, and the "all-suffering-is-a-form-of-punishment" theology is discredited. In a very real sense, God suffers *alongside* the person and is not aloof. Job's suffering is excruciating, and in the epilogue God says that unlike the three friends Job has spoken rightly of God. Because Job believes that his innocent suffering will be vindicated, some Christians and Jews have seen this passage as prefiguring heaven and hell as the only adequate explanation for the undeniable fact that sometimes good people suffer and wicked people prosper. But that is jumping ahead of our story (Chapter 6). Next we will consider one of the most hope-filled writers in the Hebrew Scriptures.

The Suffering Servant Songs of Deutero-Isaiah

During the exile in Babylon (587–539 B.C.), some Jewish men and women lost their faith and others discovered a more gracious God than they had previously known. In chapters 40–66 of the Book of Isaiah, we meet a writer intent on strengthening the faith of the exiles in Babylon. Though they may feel abandoned by God, he will intervene in human history and establish his rule over all the nations. Thus the author takes a new look at the sufferings of his Jewish contemporaries, especially in the Songs of the Suffering Servant (42:1–4; 49:1–7; 50:4–11 and 52:13–53:12).

Who is this servant? Biblical scholars suggest that the servant is both a collective personality (the nation of Israel) and an individual Messiah. In the first song, God addresses the heavenly court and describes his chosen one, his servant sent to bring forth justice to all the nations and to teach the nations. This servant combines the kingly and prophetic roles previously kept separate in Israel's history. In the second song, the servant describes his mission, raising up Israel and being a light to the nations. Though discouraged at times, the servant sees God as rewarding his labors. Here the servant seems to be a remnant of Israel enlivening the rest of the nation and announcing God's goodness to the Gentiles. Again in the third song, the servant describes himself as attentive to God's word and ready to endure insults in carrying out his mission; God will vindicate him.

In the final and longest song, God begins by saying that the servant will rise to great heights though "many people were aghast at him—he was so inhumanly disfigured that he no longer looked like a man" (v. 14). The Gentile nations then describe the servant as a sapling, a root in dry ground, "a man of sorrows, familiar with suffering" (v. 3) who bore the sufferings of others and was crushed for their guilt. "We have been healed by his bruises" (v. 5b). Like a lamb led to the slaughter, the servant is silent and opens not his mouth; he is given a grave with the wicked. In verses 11 and 12, God returns as the speaker and describes the servant's reward. His sufferings will take away the sins of many and win pardon for their offenses.

Several New Testament writers use the Suffering Servant Songs, especially the final one, as reference points for their descriptions of Jesus. These songs strengthen the idea of *redemptive* suffering endured not for one's own sins but for the sins of others.

Suffering as a Test

There are several passages in the Hebrew Scriptures, especially in the Wisdom writings, which seem to say that

God sends suffering as a means of building character. Apparently the biblical writers of these passages use a "theological shorthand" which acknowledges the suffering and immediately makes a positive interpretation of it. Then this interpretation is seen as part of God's plan all along. Although several such biblical passages could be cited, three will suffice.

When Judith addresses the elders of Bethulia making plans to defend their city against the Assyrian general Holofernes, she says:

> Brothers, let us set an example to our brothers, since their lives depend on us, and the sanctuary—Temple and altar—rests on us. All this being so, let us rather give thanks to the Lord our God who, as he tested our ancestors, is now testing us. Remember how he treated Abraham, all the ordeals of Isaac, all that happened to Jacob in Syrian Mesopotamia while he kept the sheep of Laban, his mother's brother. For as these ordeals were intended by him to search their hearts, so now this is not vengeance that God is exacting on us, but a warning inflicted by the Lord on those who are near his heart. (8:24–27)

Judith sees God's hand in all those past events though we can surely add that each person she mentions very actively participated in the story; no single reaction to "the test" was inevitable. Also, she does not mention other people who were put to "the test" and failed, e.g., Saul, Solomon and most of Israel's kings. God does not decide to "test" people by sending them suffering and then reward them for passing the test. Rather, suffering comes to everyone, and through it some people become God's martyrs while others become the "devil's martyrs." Only in that sense does God "test" us.

In the Book of Wisdom, the author ponders the suffering of just men and women who have died and says:

> If, as it seemed to us, they suffered punishment,
> their hope was rich with immortality;
> slight was their correction, great will their blessings be.
> God was putting them to the test
> and he proved them worthy to be with him;
> he has tested them like gold in a furnace,
> and accepted them as a perfect burnt offering. (3:4–6)

The author interprets the suffering of the just in a positive light and then reads back into God's will the inflicting of those sufferings. The Book of Job suggests a different sequence and does not identify God as the author of Job's sufferings.

Following God's ways and his values inevitably surfaces opposition. Thus the author of the Book of Proverbs advises:

> My child, do not scorn correction from Yahweh,
>   do not resent his reproof;
> for Yahweh reproves those he loves,
>   as a father the child whom he loves. (3:11–12)

God is no sadist sending suffering to watch how people handle it. When they choose to live by his standards, they bring some suffering on themselves. God offers grace and strength to bear that suffering and so become a witness for him and not against him. A similar theology appears at the end of the next biblical book, one of the most candid accounts in all of Scripture.

Qoheleth's Radical Questions

Qoheleth describes himself as "son of David, king in Jerusalem" (1:1). Even so, Qoheleth is almost certainly not a son of David but rather a literary convention used by a later writer, perhaps as late as 300 B.C. The Book of Qoheleth is also known as the Book of Ecclesiastes since *ecclesia* ("assembly" or "church") is the Latin equivalent for *qahal* (Hebrew for "assembly").

Qoheleth describes life as "sheer futility" (1:2). Though he has gained wisdom and has amassed wealth, Qoheleth concludes that these too are futile. Both the wise man and the fool, the rich man and the poor man, will die. So what is the use of all this striving? Treasured possessions must be left behind—perhaps to a fool. Therefore Qoheleth describes the hard work required to pile up a fortune as "futility and chasing after the wind" (2:26). There is a time for every purpose under heaven (3:1–8), even the ones diametrically opposed to each other like killing and healing. Although God has made us aware of the passing of time, "we can grasp neither the beginning nor the end of what God does" (3:11). Nevertheless, says Qoheleth, "I know there is no happiness for a human being except in pleasure and enjoyment through life" (3:12).

Man and beast both die and return to the dust; man must simply learn to rejoice in his lot. The prospects for being remembered by later generations are dim, and Qoheleth does not believe in an afterlife.

> So my conclusion is this: true happiness lies in eating and drinking and enjoying whatever has been achieved

under the sun, throughout the life given by God: for this is the lot of humanity. And whenever God gives someone riches and property, with the ability to enjoy them and to find contentment in work, this is a gift from God. For such a person will hardly notice the passing of time, so long as God keeps his heart occupied with joy. (5:17–19)

Unlike the author of Psalm 37, Qoheleth has seen "the upright person perishing in uprightness and the wicked person surviving in wickedness" (7:15). No one can "do good without ever sinning" (7:20).

> And for all of us is reserved a common fate,
> for the upright and for the wicked,
> for the good and for the bad;
> whether we are ritually pure or not,
> whether we offer sacrifice or not:
> it is the same for the good and for the sinner,
> for someone who takes a vow, as for someone who fears to
>   do so. (9:2)

In the epilogue to the Book of Qoheleth, an editor writes:

> To sum up the whole matter: fear God and keep his
>   commandments,
> for that is the duty of everyone. For God will call all our
>   deeds
> to judgement, all that is hidden, be it good or bad. (12:13–
>   14).

Theologically, Qoheleth stands between the deuteronomic tradition reflected in much of the Hebrew Scriptures and the *anawim* theology of the last two centuries before Christ, a theology which maintains that God upholds the lowly ones, the *anawim*, those who trust completely in God and who nevertheless may suffer greatly at the hands of sinners. The next chapter will explore that *anawim* theology and how the New Testament deals with innocent suffering.

For Personal Reflection

1. With which Old Testament image of God do you most identify—generous creator, wrathful lawgiver, all-knowing judge, loving parent, etc.?

2. Has this dominant image of God changed over the years? In relation to personal or family crises?

3. Can you pray with the psalmist's honesty before God? If not, would you be better off if you did pray in that manner?

4. Have you ever had a "Job" experience? Who was helpful and why? Who wasn't and why not?

5. Read the final Suffering Servant Song (Is 52:13–53:12) and pray over it during the course of a week.

6. Does God select suffering to test the faith of some people? How do you deal with the biblical passages which refer to suffering as a test sent by God?

For Group Discussion

1. Why is the deuteronomic theology so appealing?

2. There is a great temptation to absolutize our earliest images of God. How can we grow toward more adult images of God?

3. How do you deal with the fact that following God's ways often causes suffering for the disciple?

4. If offering the "comfort" of Job's friends does not work, what does?

5. In what way is "redemptive suffering" the opposite of being one of "the devil's martyrs"?

6. The rabbis once debated whether Qoheleth should be included in the Hebrew Scriptures. Some said it is too pessimistic. Is it? What would be lost if it had not been included in the Scriptures?

Resources

1. John L. McKenzie, *The Two-Edged Sword: An Interpretation of the Old Testament* (Bruce, 1956). Chapter 12 is entitled "The Mystery of Iniquity."

2. Renee Rust, O.S.B., *Praying the Biblical Psalms— Then Praying Your Own,* an audiocassette series from St. Anthony Messenger Press, 1985. A helpful study guide is included.

3. Elizabeth and Paul Achtemeier, *The Old Testament Roots of Our Faith* (Fortress, 1962).

4. Claus Westermann, *What Does the Old Testament Say About God?* (John Knox Press, 1979).

3

Innocent Suffering
According to the New Testament

The question of innocent suffering occurs in the New Testament mostly in terms of the sufferings of Jesus and those of his first-century disciples. This chapter will sample that theology of innocent suffering by focusing on two teachings of Jesus and will then highlight the *anawim* (poor of Yahweh) theology, the Gospel of Matthew on discipleship, Romans, 2 Corinthians, Colossians, 1 Peter and the Book of Revelation. Several New Testament texts will be utilized in later chapters.

When Jesus set out to announce conversion and the reign of God, some of his Jewish listeners still believed that suffering was a sign of God's punishment. Many of his pagan listeners were well acquainted with basically cruel gods (Chapter 4). Breaking those old thought patterns and introducing his disciples to the abundant, saving love of a God they could call "Father" challenged Jesus throughout his public ministry.

Two Teachings of Jesus

Jesus makes only two very direct comments on innocent suffering in general (that is, apart from his own suffer-

ing and that which flows from discipleship), but both incidents can teach us a great deal.

In the Gospel of John, Jesus meets a man blind from
birth. When the disciples ask "Rabbi, who sinned, this man
or his parents, that he should have been born blind?" Jesus
answers:

> Neither he nor his parents sinned.
> He was born blind
> so that the works of God might be revealed in him.
> As long as day lasts
> we must carry out the work of the one who sent me;
> the night will soon be here when no one can work.
> As long as I am in the world
> I am the light of the world. (9:3–5)

In a sense, the disciples' question reflects the deuteronomic
theology; this tragic blindness flows from someone's sin—
the man's or his parents'. Jesus quickly denies their either/
or question, bypasses the whole issue of how sin and physical illness may be related, and instead says that this man's
blindness allows God's saving power to assert itself. This
cure is another of Jesus' "signs" which strengthen the faith
of disciples but remain a puzzle to all others. When the
newly-cured man explains what has happened to him, the
Pharisees respond, "Are you trying to teach us, and you a
sinner through and through ever since you were born?"
(9:34). Job's comforters are alive and well, protecting their
self-serving theology by all available means.

Throughout this episode the evangelist plays on the
irony of the cured blind man and the Pharisees who are
blind to what Jesus is doing. In some ways Jesus' disciples
echo the theology of Job's friends—certainly the Pharisees
do. "God punished you" summarizes their best explanation

of why this man cannot see. In this Gospel incident, however, Jesus clearly rejects the idea that suffering automatically indicates some sin committed by the one suffering or
his/her ancestors. Shaming the victim into silence is not a
Gospel solution.

In the Gospel of Luke, Jesus responds to a question of
innocent suffering by recalling Pilate's punishment of some
Galileans. Unfortunately, when most Christians think of
Pilate, they remember only his seemingly passive role in
the death of Jesus. Rarely do they remember this scene:

> It was just about this time that some people arrived and
> told him [Jesus] about the Galileans whose blood Pilate
> had mingled with that of their sacrifices. At this he said
> to them, 'Do you suppose that these Galileans were
> worse sinners than any others, that this should have
> happened to them? They were not, I tell you. No; but
> unless you repent you will all perish as they did. Or
> those eighteen on whom the tower at Siloam fell, killing
> them all? Do you suppose that they were more guilty
> than all the other people living in Jerusalem? They
> were not, I tell you. No; but unless you repent you will
> all perish as they did.' (13:1–5)

Once again, Jesus does not explain innocent suffering, but
he clearly rejects one popular explanation of it—a sure
indication of personal guilt. Everyone must repent while
there is still time.

The Poor of Yahweh Theology

The Gospel of Luke has sometimes been called the
"Gospel of the Poor" because its author stresses Jesus'
mission to all God's people, rich and poor, and because this

Gospel sums up several centuries of *anawim* (poor of Yahweh) theology. The "poor" here are materially poor as well as "poor in spirit." Observing God's law they seek justice and humility (Zeph 2:3). They trust completely that God will be faithful to his promises, that those who follow God's ways and suffer for them are not foolish. The *anawim* represent the "remnant" whose faith grows even when the Jews live under pagan rulers; they joyfully await the Lord's heavenly banquet (Is 55:1–13).

Luke's "poor of Yahweh" theology comes into sharpest focus through the women and men of his infancy narrative: Zechariah and Elizabeth, Mary and Joseph, Simeon and Anna in the temple—all devout, humble Jews who have faithfully observed the exterior law of Moses while also converting to the Lord continuously. Luke's shepherds in Bethlehem are unable to observe all the Mosaic dietary laws, but Jesus comes for them also. Thus these *anawim* stand ready to take their part in God's plan of salvation. The "poor of Yahweh" theology reaches its summit in Mary's canticle proclaiming that God's mercy is from age to age on those who fear him (1:50). Those who trust in God and seek his justice will not be disappointed.

Luke's *anawim* theology explains the more simple version of the first beatitude ("Blessed are you poor") and two parables unique to Luke (Lazarus and the rich man, and the rich man who built larger grain bins). This theology can be found in other New Testament writings, especially in the Letter of James.

The *anawim* know innocent human suffering from firsthand experience, but they have passed beyond the "suffering-as-punishment" theology and fully expect God to uphold his faithful ones. Theirs is a spirit of Gospel repentance and hope in the kingdom of God.

Innocent Suffering/Discipleship in Matthew's Gospel

Not only does Jesus *not* explain innocent suffering arising from the forces of nature or an abuse of human freedom, but he presumes that his disciples will be quite familiar with the suffering caused by other people.

Jesus opens the Sermon on the Mount (chapters 5–7)
with eight beatitudes, each one a form of innocent suffering
inevitably arising from the choice to follow Jesus. Throughout the Sermon, Jesus urges his listeners to go beyond the
surface requirements of the Mosaic law and serve God and
each other with an increasingly generous love. For example, after quoting the commandment "Eye for eye and
tooth for tooth," Jesus says:

> But I say this to you: offer no resistance to the wicked.
> On the contrary, if anyone hits you on the right cheek,
> offer him the other as well; if someone wishes to go to
> law with you to get your tunic, let him have your cloak
> as well. And if anyone requires you to go one mile, go
> two miles with him. Give to anyone who asks you, and
> if anyone wants to borrow, do not turn away. (5:39–42)

The disciples' prayer and fasting should represent an ever-
deeper harmony with God; for this reason, the disciples
must be open to conversion, to seeing the "great log" in
one's own eye rather than the splinter in someone else's
(7:1–5). Jesus summarizes the Sermon by comparing the
person who does the Father's will to the man who built his
house on solid rock.

When Jesus sends the twelve apostles on their first
missionary journey, he describes the hostile reception they
may receive. Indeed, he sends them "like sheep among
wolves" (10:16). Though families will be divided over the
good news, according to Jesus, "Anyone who does not take

his cross and follow in my footsteps is not worthy of me" (v. 38).

But the wisdom of the cross takes root only with difficulty. After Jesus has identified Peter as the "rock" on which he will build the community, Jesus predicts his passion, death and resurrection, prompting Peter to argue with Jesus and say: "Heaven preserve you, Lord. This must not happen to you" (16:22). Jesus immediately turns to Peter and says: "Get behind me, Satan! You are an obstacle in my path, because you are thinking not as God thinks but as human beings do" (16:23). Though Peter views innocent suffering as a sign of shame and defeat, Jesus turns those standards upside down. Peter's understanding of discipleship ripens slowly. In time he follows Jesus literally to the cross.

Immediately after Jesus' third prediction of his coming death and resurrection, the mother of James and John tries to win special places for her sons in Jesus' kingdom. When the other apostles begin to grumble, Jesus tells them that unlike Gentile authorities who make their importance felt, authority in his kingdom is related to humble service. Indeed, the Son of Man will give his own life as a "ransom for the many" (20:28).

Later Jesus compares the reign of God to the wise bridesmaids who provided oil for their lamps and thus were ready for the wedding, no matter at what unpredictable hour the bridegroom came. Or the reign of God is like the man who distributed money to his servants, went away, and on returning demanded an accounting. The servant who had been unwilling to risk failure and thus hid the money receives a harsh judgment.

Isn't the Last Judgment scene (25:31–46) really about innocent suffering? Those who are saved do not seem to see feeding the hungry, clothing the naked, etc., as acts of charity done to God. That's simply how people should treat one another. Likewise, those condemned in this scene are surprised that God makes such a big deal out of not helping those seemingly insignificant people. Perhaps those condemned had rationalized that the hungry and homeless really "had it coming to them" anyway because they lacked initiative and hustle. Maybe those condemned saw hunger and nakedness as "God's will" for those other people!

Only innocent suffering explains the prayer of Jesus in the Garden of Gethsemane, "My Father, if it is possible, let this cup pass me by. Nevertheless, let it be as you, not I, would have it" (26:39). If the perfectly sinless Son of God died on the cross, his followers can hardly be strangers to innocent suffering.

As Jesus dies on that cross, his suffering is used as a proof of his guilt. Bystanders jeer, "Save yourself if you are God's Son and come down from the cross!" (27:40). In fact, only God's Son could have drunk this chalice of suffering until the very end. Who could believe, many asked themselves, in a Messiah hanging on a cross, subjected to the most degrading form of execution employed by the Romans? The passion, death and resurrection of Jesus confirm all his parables, his miracles, his teachings about discipleship—in short, the wisdom of the cross.

Romans

To the Christian community in Rome, known to him only by reputation, Paul addresses a long letter on the relationship of Judaism and Christianity, explaining the divine plan of salvation in what otherwise appears as a very confusing situation.

According to Paul, all people have sinned and have been deprived of God's glory; likewise, all of us "are justified by the free gift of his grace through being set free in Christ Jesus" (3:24). Abraham, the father of all believers, was saved not simply through observing the Mosaic law but by trusting that God would fulfill his promises. Indeed,

> When we were still helpless, at the appointed time, Christ died for the godless. You could hardly find any-one ready to die even for someone upright, though it is just possible that, for a really good person, someone might undertake to die. So it is proof of God's own love for us, that Christ died for us while we were still sin-ners. (5:6–8)

Such love prompts Paul to ask the Roman Christians:

> Can anything cut us off from the love of Christ—can hardship or distress, or persecution, or lack of food and clothing, or threats or violence? As scripture says, 'For your sake we are being massacred all day long, treated as sheep to be slaughtered.' No; we come through all these things triumphantly victorious, by the power of him who loved us. For I am certain of this: neither death nor life, nor angels, nor principalities, nothing already in existence and nothing still to come, nor any power, nor the heights nor the depths, nor any created thing whatever, will be able to come between us and the love of God, known to us in Christ Jesus our Lord. (8:35–39)

Innocent suffering is certainly no stranger to Christ's fol-lowers, but it cannot be allowed to cast Christ's redeeming death and resurrection into doubt. The Christians in Rome are to offer their bodies as a living sacrifice acceptable to God. "Do not model your behaviour on the contemporary world, but let the renewing of your minds transform you, so that you may discern for yourselves what is the will of God—what is good and acceptable and mature" (12:2). Paul urges the Roman Christians to bless their persecutors. "Do not be mastered by evil, but master evil with good" (12:21).

2 Corinthians

Perhaps in no other letter does Paul describe so personally all the joys and hardships he has experienced in preaching the Gospel; other Christians can expect a similar sharing in the paschal mystery. The letter opens with "Paul, by the will of God an apostle of Christ Jesus" (1:1).

In the New Testament we find the expression "the will of God" fifteen times, eight times in the writings of Paul. Only three times in the New Testament is God's will linked to suffering (1 Peter below). The expression "will of God" appears only once in the Hebrew Scriptures and then in a context of healing when the angel Raphael says that he has come to Tobit's family "by the will of God" (12:18).

After wishing the Corinthians grace and peace from God our Father and the Lord Jesus Christ, Paul prays:

Blessed be the God and Father of our Lord Jesus Christ, the merciful Father and the God who gives every possible encouragement; he supports us in every hardship, so that we are able to come to the support of others, in every hardship of theirs because of the encouragement that we ourselves receive from God. For just as the sufferings of Christ overflow into our lives, so too does the encouragement we receive through Christ. So if we have hardships to undergo, this will contribute to your encouragement and your salvation; if we receive encouragement, this is to gain for you the encouragement which enables you to bear with perse-

verance the same sufferings as we do. So our hope for
you is secure in the knowledge that you share the encouragement we receive, no less than the sufferings we
bear. (1:3–7)

Sharing in Christ's sufferings should lead us to share with
others the compassion God has shown to us. Suffering need
not destroy hope.

Paul writes this letter to explain his apostolic ministry
to the Church in Corinth and to answer several accusations
made against that ministry (especially that Paul, not one of
the twelve apostles, is a minor witness to Jesus). Rather,
says Paul:

> It is not ourselves that we are proclaiming, but Christ
> Jesus as the Lord, and ourselves as your servants for
> Jesus' sake. It is God who said, 'Let light shine out of
> darkness,' that has shone into our hearts to enlighten
> them with the knowledge of God's glory, the glory on
> the face of Christ. But we hold this treasure in pots of
> earthenware, so that the immensity of the power is
> God's and not our own. We are subjected to every
> kind of hardship, but never distressed; we see no way
> out but we never despair; we are pursued but never
> cut off; knocked down, but still have some life in us;
> always we carry with us in our body the death of Jesus
> so that the life of Jesus, too, may be visible in our
> body. (4:5–10)

Christ died for us, says Paul, that we might live not for
ourselves but for him who died for us and was raised up to
life (5:15).

> From now onwards, then, we will not consider anyone
> by human standards: even if we were once familiar with

Christ according to human standards, we do not know him in that way any longer. So for anyone who is in Christ, there is a new creation: the old order is gone and a new being is there to see. It is all God's work; he reconciled us to himself through Christ and he gave us the ministry of reconciliation. I mean, God was in Christ reconciling the world to himself, not holding anyone's faults against them, but entrusting to us the message of reconciliation. So we are ambassadors for Christ; it is as though God were urging you through us, and in the name of Christ we appeal to you to be reconciled to God. For our sake he made the sinless one a victim for sin, so that in him we might become the uprightness of God. (5:16–21)

Our sharing in the passion, death and resurrection of Jesus should undergird a ministry of reconciliation, a ministry which includes reaching out to all those beaten down by suffering interpreted as "God's will" and a sign of his displeasure. "God's will," says Paul in another letter, is rather that we be holy and give thanks to God for all things (1 Thes 4:3; 5:18).

Paul details for the Corinthian Christians all the sufferings he has endured as an apostle (especially 6:1–10 and 11:1–33), but all of this counts little in comparison to the unspeakable joy which God has revealed to him. Nevertheless, Paul reveals:

Wherefore, so that I should not get above myself, I was given a thorn in the flesh, a messenger from Satan to batter me and prevent me from getting above myself. About this, I have three times pleaded with the Lord that it might leave me; but he has answered me, 'My grace is enough for you: for power is at full strength in weakness.' It is, then, about my weaknesses that I am happiest of all to boast, so that the power of Christ may rest upon me. (12:7–9)

If the apostle Paul, an extraordinary preacher of God's word, encountered harsh physical sufferings and emotional fatigue from backbiting rivals, and yet could remain so enthusiastic and hopeful, can any follower of Jesus expect a life free from suffering? Similarly, can every faithful Christian expect the same joy Paul indicated? Assuredly.

Anyone interested in more of Paul's reflections on his sufferings and on the hope in God animating his ministry should read the Letter to the Philippians, written while Paul was in prison, unsure whether he would be sentenced to death. No sad farewell letter here—only the strong recommendation to imitate his faith and trust in God.

Is Anything Lacking in the Sufferings of Christ?

In his Letter to the Colossians, Paul writes to a church in which some members see Jesus Christ as simply one of many heavenly beings who control creation and whose favor can be cultivated by observing special feast days and also special fast days. Paul responds by asserting Christ's primacy over all creation, the divine leadership of the Church and Christ's position as "first-born from the dead." The Colossian Christians should be firmly grounded in faith and unshaken in the hope promised by the Gospel. "It makes me happy," says Paul, "to be suffering for you now, and in my own body to make up all the hardships that still have to be undergone by Christ for the sake of his body, the Church" (1:24).

How does Paul "make up" those hardships? How do other Christians share in that mission? One explanation is that preaching the Gospel (either explicitly as Paul does or

implicitly through Gospel-based living as all the baptized
do) always causes division because some people receive it
with joy and others do not. Persecution often follows.
Some hardships await all Christians and must be endured
until the good news has been preached to every person.
Many of the sufferings which Christians face can be
avoided only by denying their baptism and its consequences. Such hardships will not account for all innocent
suffering (e.g., if the parents of a newborn child with
Down's syndrome ask "Why us, Lord?"), but it explains
some cases (e.g., the honest person who sees dishonesty
apparently pay off for someone else).

Is It Ever God's Will That We Suffer?

Much of the New Testament was written for Christians
who accepted the good news with joy and enthusiasm and
only later realized that following Jesus would force them to
make several very deep and painful choices. Abandoning
that Gospel could, for example, remove the possibility of
martyrdom and would certainly allow them to "get ahead"
more quickly. The First Letter of Peter was written for just
such Christians, unsure of what their baptism means in
daily life. After praising the God who has given them birth
to a "heritage that can never be spoilt or soiled and never
fade away" (1:4), the author says:

> This is a great joy to you, even though for a short time
> yet you must bear all sorts of trials; so that the worth of
> your faith, more valuable than gold, which is perishable
> even if it has been tested by fire, may be proved—to
> your praise and honour when Jesus Christ is revealed.
> (1:6–7)

Christians who have never met Jesus love and believe in him; they have been delivered from a futile way of life by the precious blood "of a blameless and spotless lamb, Christ" (1:19). Since God has called them "out of the darkness into his wonderful light" (2:9), they should live as free men and women, not using their freedom as a cover for wickedness (2:16).

The author then urges slaves to obey their masters and accept any suffering which may arise from doing what is right, as Christ did. "He [Christ] was bearing our sins in his own body on the cross, so that we might die to our sins and live for uprightness; through his bruises you have been healed" (2:24). Later the author explains, "And if it is the will of God that you should suffer, it is better to suffer for doing right than for doing wrong" (3:17).

Certainly the author indicates here God's *permissive* will (what he allows to happen) rather than his *active* will (e.g., creating men and women because he wants to share divine life with them). But people have sometimes misinterpreted language such as 1 Peter 3:17 uses; thus God becomes a sadist, enjoying pain inflicted on others. The same difficulty can arise with 1 Peter 4:19, "So even those whom God allows to suffer should commit themselves to a Creator who is trustworthy, and go on doing good." God does not protect Christians from all persecution (then or now) arising from human malice, but God remains steadfastly faithful and loving.

Simply a Book of Strange Visions and Puzzling Symbols?

Few Christians would identify the Book of Revelation (also known as the Apocalypse) as their favorite New Testament writing. On first reading or hearing some passages, many Christians find the visions bizarre and the imagery (especially the numbers) very confusing. Hearing that this book arises from profound Christian hope would strike such Christians as very odd. And yet this book was written precisely to encourage followers of Jesus who might die for their faith. Apocalyptic literature (e.g., Ezekiel and Daniel in the Hebrew Scriptures) arises during times of great communal suffering.

Though Scripture scholars differ on the exact dating of the Book of Revelation, many suggest the fierce persecution under Domitian (81–96 A.D.) who insisted on being called "Dominus," the Latin equivalent for "Kyrios" (Lord). The New Testament's final book stubbornly affirms that Jesus is Lord and that God will prevail even amid the harshest persecution of Christians. At every turn the Book of Revelation presents God's ways as ultimately victorious despite appearances to the contrary. In a sense, God suffers *with* his people; he doesn't *send* suffering to test their loyalty.

Misusing the Scriptures About Suffering

From what has been presented here and in the previous chapter, we can see that the Hebrew Scriptures and the New Testament do not promote a tidy but ultimately heartless theology which sees all suffering as punishment for the individual's sins or those of his/her ancestors. Though some suffering is unexplained (men killed by the falling tower in Siloam), God's providence is steadfastly affirmed. "God punished you" may be a popular expression, but that phrase reveals more about the speaker than about God.

The Scriptures should make us slow to identify all suffering as "God's will." God does not "will" that the hungry and the naked remain hungry and naked (Mt 25). God "wills" that people respond to such needs with compassion. Most evil happens through an abuse of human freedom. The man going from Jerusalem to Jericho fell among robbers and was left half-dead. A priest and a levite ignored his need; only the Samaritan, a stranger in this territory, saw this man as "neighbor." God intended that the priest, the levite and the Samaritan all have a very wide notion of "neighbor" and be ready to sacrifice themselves for the sake of someone in need. But only the Good Samaritan acted on God's will. God's grace and human freedom cooperated magnificently only in the Good Samaritan's response.

A misuse of the Scriptures could lead us to accept the deuteronomic theology in a distorted manner and so offer suffering men, women and children the cruel comfort of Job's friends. The next chapter will consider the dangers which arise from careless talk (and resulting harsh actions) concerning "God's will."

For Personal Reflection

1. Does being a disciple of Jesus inevitably lead to suffering? What kind of suffering?

2. Have I considered the Beatitudes as heroic practices for super-disciples or the daily consequences of following Jesus?

3. Who or what separates me from the love of Christ (Rom 8)? What can I do about that?

4. Jesus has entrusted the ministry of reconciliation to each one of us (2 Cor 5). How can I exercise that ministry today?

5. Does the author's distinction between God's active will and his permissive will make sense to me? Why or why not?

6. Have I heard people speak carelessly about "God's will"? Have I done so?

For Group Discussion

1. What does Mary the Mother of Jesus tell us about innocent suffering?
2. How do we move from judging by man's standards to judging by God's standards (Mt 16)? What do we have to put aside? To take up?
3. Most of Jesus' contemporaries saw the cross as a proof of his defeat; a few of them saw it as a sign of triumph. Did God reveal the mystery of the cross to some and not to others? Or is there another explanation?
4. Paul tells the Romans to "conquer evil with good." Give examples of that on the personal, family, civic and parish level.
5. Why does suffering sometimes lead to compassion and at other times to selfishness?
6. In what sense is it "God's will" that disciples suffer? How are "God's will" and human freedom connected?

Resources

1. John L. McKenzie, *The Power and the Wisdom: An Interpretation of the New Testament* (Bruce, 1965). See Chapters VI ("Saving Act of Jesus") and XI ("Christian Moral Revolution") especially.
2. Karen Berry, O.S.F., *Beyond Broken Dreams: A Scriptural Pathway to New Life* (St. Anthony Messenger Press, 1985).
3. Johannes B. Metz, *Poverty of Spirit* (Paulist, 1968).

4. Donald Senior, C.P., *An Invitation to Matthew* (Doubleday, 1977).

5. Raymond Brown, S.S., *The Churches the Apostles Left Behind* (Paulist, 1984).

6. Pat Sena, C.PP.S., *The Apocalypse: Biblical Revelation Explained,* a book by Alba House (1983) and an audiocassette series from St. Anthony Messenger Press (1984).

7. Bertrand Buby, S.M., *Mary the Faithful Disciple* (Paulist, 1985).

4

Do You Believe in a Cruel God?

In Verdi's opera *Otello,* Iago makes a blasphemous profession of faith when he sings "Credo in un Dio crudel" (I believe in a cruel God). A cruel God intended that humans be cruel; not surprisingly, Iago remains for many readers the most despicable character in Western literature. Shakespeare presents him, in effect, as a parasite destroying other people's reputations by his lies and innuendos. Iago is more pathetic than tragic, without any hint of a gift gone sour and eventually self-destructive. Understanding the tragic flaws of Macbeth, Lear or Othello seems child's play; Iago defies comprehension. Considering him the devil incarnate seems the best solution.

But Iago's chilling *credo* will not go away, for I believe it explains how Christians can become great countersigns of the good news—"the devil's martyrs," to use Soelle's expression. In fact, they can believe in a cruel God—or act that way—even if they would vigorously deny the suggestion. Indeed, they can even appear very religious, very devout.

Did Iago always believe in a cruel God? Highly unlikely. More probably, he believed in a compassionate God until one day he found himself suffering innocently, only to be met with the self-serving theology of Job's friends. Unlike Job, however, Iago probably seemed to accept this careless "will of God" explanation, all the while denying it internally. Did Iago deny his feelings of anger at God until one day he realized he could not worship a God so indifferent to human suffering? How many people like Iago secretly believe in a cruel God or are heading in that direction? Too many, I'm afraid, if the number I've met gives any indication.

In this connection, Nicholas Lash offers valuable advice for the possible direction of Catholic theology today:

> Perhaps only a faith that has lost its nerve feels obliged continually to insist that it is quite sure of itself, that it knows quite clearly what is to be said concerning the mystery of God. This is by no means merely a theoretical issue. If the tone of our theological and ecclesiastical discourse were to become again more contemplatively unsure of *itself,* more the voice of prayer and hope, less cognitively and institutionally self-assertive, then we will find it more difficult than we have sometimes done in the recent past to speak glibly and uncomplicatedly about the "will of God," the "law of God," and so on. Immense human suffering has been caused by people who, lacking any profound understanding of themselves, were nevertheless quite confident that they understood God. (*Theology on Dover Beach*)

Unfortunately, Iago's blasphemy and its modern counterparts may be one way of rejecting careless talk about "God's will." Two groups especially in New Testament times thought they understood "God's will," yet their ideas undermined—and continue to undermine—the good news of Jesus Christ.

Pharisaism: Jewish and Christian Varieties

Yes, there are Christian Pharisees even if we may identify that term exclusively with Judaism. But first the Jewish variety.

Although Job's friends were not Pharisees, their ideas about the relation of God's law, human sinfulness, divine punishment and repentance resemble the theology favored by the Pharisees, a theology which can easily lead non-Pharisees to conclude that God is cruel. In fact, many Pharisees suspected the same though they hid it very well. Remember their explanation (Chapter 3) for why the man Jesus cured was born blind?

Admittedly the Gospels do not give a completely objective account of the Pharisee movement; the Gospel most opposed to Pharisaism (Matthew) was written after the Palestinian Pharisees began to exclude Jewish Christians from synagogue worship. As it became more obvious that Christianity was much more than a sect within Judaism, the parting of the ways brought great pain to many Jewish Christians. Even so, the Gospels' generally negative portrayal of the Pharisees is supported by other Jewish and pagan sources from that period.

The Gospel Pharisees are often self-righteous schemers willing to align themselves with anyone (even the hated Sadducees, Rome's Jewish insiders) to get rid of Jesus, a challenge to their teaching authority. But their prayer and fasting were frequently for show, and their legalism has become legendary. How could they have made any positive contribution to Judaism? Understanding their strength may help us to understand their weakness.

Of the four main groups within Judaism at the time of Jesus (Sadducees, Pharisees, Zealots and Essenes), the Pharisees have certainly had the greatest influence in shaping Judaism through the centuries. When Solomon's temple was destroyed in 587 B.C., the Hebrew people lost their religious focal point. The ensuing national examination of conscience led some people to locate Jewish identity in knowing and following the law of Moses. By the time the temple was rebuilt, many Jews lived so far from Jerusalem that they could go to the temple only for the major feasts. Thus for most Jews synagogues and rabbis became more important than temple worship and leadership by the priestly family. The Pharisees (the name means "separate") urged Jews not to mingle with the Gentile world on its terms or they would cease being Jewish—as some did. Pharisaism emerges as a fully organized movement only around 140 B.C. though its roots go back farther. They emphasized education and believed in oral tradition, the resurrection of the body and the coming of a Messiah.

Eventually, however, Pharisaism and legalism became interchangeable words. Jesus criticizes them for observing the most minute details of the law while neglecting such fundamentals as justice and mercy (Mt 23:23). The law can protect a person from God. Although we may not think of Pharisees as being angry at God, I suspect that deep down many of them in Jesus' day shared such anger which was displaced onto less zealous observers of the law. An apparently chaotic world run by godless Gentiles can be made intelligible through carefully observing "the law" and condemning those less zealous. Eventually the Pharisees saw "God's will" in great detail: this evil happened because the law was disregarded; that blessing is a reward for observing the law. Self-righteousness comes easily under such circumstances. Certainly the Pharisee praying in the front of the temple (Lk 18) enjoys his success at following the law. But doesn't his self-congratulatory prayer suggest a polite anger at God? Some slight fear that God might not be as impressed by fasting and tithing as the Pharisee is? Strong words can cover self-doubt.

Isn't the Pharisee praying in the temple really engaged in subtle idolatry—worshiping himself while pretending to worship a God so concerned with little rules? Why is Jesus fond of quoting Hosea 6:6 ("Faithful love is what pleases me, not sacrifice")? Why did Judaizing Christians (very easily former Pharisees) constantly undermine Paul's mission to the Gentiles by suggesting that baptism should be linked with circumcision and the Mosaic dietary laws? Who (or what) is the Pharisee worshiping?

Pharisaic zeal often fosters Pharisaic anger, as the parable of the prodigal son (Lk 15:11–32) demonstrates.

Chapter 15 of Luke's Gospel presents three parables of divine mercy: the shepherd leaving the ninety-nine to find the one lost sheep, the woman searching for her lost silver piece and the story of the prodigal son. But notice how these parables are introduced: "The tax collectors and sinners, however, were all crowding round to listen to him [Jesus], and the Pharisees and scribes complained saying, 'This man welcomes sinners and eats with them" (15:1–2). God's joy over repenting sinners pushes aside the Pharisees' need to balance the account books and make sure that everyone has paid fully for all the offenses committed.

How many prodigal son sermons have you heard? What was emphasized? Probably that the younger son came to his senses (repented) and that the father was very generous in forgiving. True, but how many times have you heard a sermon which squarely faced the elder brother's anger and self-righteousness? How easily we identify with the prodigal son or the forgiving father, but how often have we seen ourselves in the elder brother's role? Probably not often, yet that is the whole point of the parable. The elder brother has served the father conscientiously but grudgingly. After bitterly recalling his own hard work without even a kid goat to celebrate with his friends, the elder brother adds venomously: "But, for this son of yours, when he comes back after swallowing up your property—he and his loose women—you kill the calf we had been fattening" (v. 30). The elder brothers says "this son of yours"—not "my brother." He also twists the knife in his father's back by interpreting the prodigal's bankruptcy in extremely vivid terms.

Defending himself, the father replies that the younger son "was dead and has come to life; he was lost and is found" (v. 32). But the exact opposite can be said of the elder brother: he seemed alive (hard work!) but is now dead (killed by unresolved anger masking as piety); he seemed to "have his act together" but is now lost in the fog of self-righteousness. If he ever "comes to his senses" (v. 17), the elder brother will see how his puny self-righteousness pales before God's mercy. Religion can help angry people seem very respectable, but no religious group can prevent self-righteous anger from destroying the person from within. Only repentance can reverse this dry rot, and yet this cure is unlikely to be accepted because, after all, it is the sinners (non-observers of my cozy laws) who need to be cured.

Has Pharisaism died away? Was it a uniquely first-century Jewish phenomenon? Hardly. Christians can and have developed their own "righteousness," their own "inside track" with God, their own safeguards to control a careless God who might not do the right thing. When one person tries to control someone else (another person or God), we don't call that "love." Anger, not love, motivates self-righteous men and women (Jews, Christians, whoever, first century or any century) to try putting God in their debt; zeal can successfully camouflage anger. Exact observance can mean that God has no claim on me; indeed, I have a huge claim on God. "I was hurt once and I'm never going to be hurt that way again" could describe many Pharisees scrupulously observing self-imposed laws.

Where is Pharisaism active among Christians today? Take your pick: people who see AIDS as God's clear judgment on homosexuality (never mind that others can and have contracted the disease); people who believe in chain letters or that praying a certain prayer a certain number of times will guarantee salvation; people who believe that God is a rather harsh judge but the Virgin Mary can sneak her clients into heaven through the back gate; people who too readily thank God that they "are not like the rest of man—grasping, crooked, adulterous—or even like this tax collector [substitute your favorite despised person or group]" (Lk 18:11)—in short, anyone who feels confident of having the "inside track" with God and an "enemies' list" which matches God's exactly.

Satan, the father of lies, encourages us to believe in a cruel God yet deny that. Self-righteous anger is truly diabolic because life is drained from a person who still seems very zealous and at times heroic.

Stoicism's Cruel God

Stoicism, the most popular pagan philosophy at the time of Jesus, suggested that people suffer because they do not control their emotions. The self-sufficient Stoic must conform himself to nature and consider apathy (lack of feeling) as the highest virtue. Human beings contain a spark of divine life imprisoned in a body. Stoicism emphasizes duty, the natural law and the radical equality of all people; its ideal of self-sufficiency can easily foster an excessive individualism. Like Pharisaism, Stoicism continues to flourish, even among believers.

The pagan Stoic sees the world as a single living being whose soul is Nature (God). Each part exists for the whole and has no meaning by itself. If the Stoic recognizes his/her insignificance, the resulting indifference to pain and pleasure will lead to self-sufficiency. Though Stoicism had a wide appeal in Jesus' day, more wealthy men and women had an easier time believing in their own self-sufficiency. Even so, one of the greatest Stoic philosophers was the Roman slave Epictetus.

For the Stoics any personal happiness is muted by a strong sense of individual fragility; pain is made bearable by identifying its cause (not respecting nature's laws); fortunately, pain's remedy (self-control) lies within the grasp of each person. Emotions are automatically dangerous and must therefore be disciplined. Since blind fate rules everyone, a certain passivity results. If life still becomes too difficult, the Stoic (denying any afterlife) should commit suicide. Stoicism's God is very perfect, very aloof and—to be honest—rather cruel. Though Christians may consider a cruel God a contradiction in terms, the ancient world knew many cruel gods.

Fine. But what does Stoicism have to do with Christianity? When some Stoics became Christians, they naturally reinterpreted some of their previous beliefs, but not always enough to appreciate what makes Jesus' good news unique. The "natural law" terminology quickly found a home in Christianity. Learning "God's will" (about what career I should follow, whether I should marry this person or not, etc.) assumed greater urgency. Regrettably, an unhealthy passivity began to look virtuous. Penitential practices can keep the emotions from wreaking their inevitable havoc; naturally, Stoics do not get angry.

Eventually the Stoic reinterpretation of Christianity threatened to crowd out the biblical revelation on salvation, grace, freedom in Christ and the enslaving power of sin. God became very distant and somewhat indifferent to human suffering. Thus prayers must catch his attention and inform him about minor details he may have overlooked in the running of an immense universe.

Puritan anger, Jansenistic scrupulosity and perhaps even fundamentalist rigidity are probably more indebted to Stoicism than to the New Testament. Other people threaten to contaminate my relationship with God; spiritual self-sufficiency sees "the world" only in the New Testament's negative use of that term. The Bible's positive sense of that term (the place of our encounter with God) can easily be forgotten. Stoicism was almost in the air that first-century pagans breathed; in many ways it's in the air that twentieth-century Americans breathe. When little boys are urged not to cry but rather "act like a man," the basic message is Stoic. When people believe that "getting ahead" is all that counts, it is Stoic self-sufficiency pulling those strings.

Stoics (ancient and modern, Christian and otherwise) can easily identify evil with some person or group (e.g., the men and women executed in Salem, Massachusetts on charges of witchcraft). Holiness means becoming like angels. A very ruthless discipline can look zealous since Stoic Christians tend to see most human suffering as solved by greater self-discipline. They may even complain when religious groups become too "political" (that is, threaten my self-sufficiency).

Atheism: One Answer to Stoicism and Pharisaism

I believe that Christian Pharisaism and Christian Stoicism continue to undermine the basic Judaeo-Christian revelation and thus nurture belief in a cruel God. If people revolt against the Pharisaic or Stoic versions of Christianity, they can easily conclude that they are "losing their faith" when, in fact, they may be drawing closer to a key revelation of Jesus: that God is Father and desires that every person be saved (reconciled to God and to one another) and share in the eternal banquet to which all are invited. Iago's chilling *credo* caught my attention because it said succinctly what I had heard more vaguely in several confessional or counseling situations.

Christians reluctant to ask God (and themselves!) hard questions often fear "losing" a faith which they identify with the Pharisaic or Stoic image of God. Living with constant, low-grade anger at God may seem the only alternative to atheism. But is it? When the bishops at Vatican II turned their attention to contemporary atheism, they identified its various roots and manifestations. Some atheists, they said,

> have such a faulty notion of God that when they disown this product of their imagination their denial has no reference to the God of the Gospels. . . . Not infrequently atheism is born from a violent protest against evil in the world, or from the fact that certain human ideals are wrongfully invested with such an absolute character as to be taken for God. (*Pastoral Constitution on the Church in the Modern World*, §19)

Pharisaism? Stoicism? They certainly claim an absolute character. The bishops then admit that believers share some responsibility for the growth of atheism:

For atheism, taken as a whole, is not present in the
mind of man from the start. It springs from various
causes, among which must be included a critical reaction against religions and, in some places, against the
Christian religion in particular. Believers can thus have
more than a little to do with the rise of atheism. To the
extent that they are careless about their instruction in
the faith, or present its teaching falsely, or even fail in
their religious, moral or social life, they must be said to
conceal rather than reveal the true nature of God and
of religion. (§19)

Jesus invites the men and women who follow him to an
adult faith—not the immature faith of Christian Pharisaism
or Christian Stoicism, but a mature faith centered on the
Lord's passion, death and resurrection. Such faith reminds
us of our sinfulness, the sufferings of others and the ever-
present divine grace which nurtures a compassion like the
Good Samaritan's. To the extent that Christians accept and
live out a mature faith, the number of witnesses in favor of
a cruel God ("the devil's martyrs") will decrease and human suffering will become less likely to foster atheism.

For Personal Reflection

1. How does it happen that some people believe in a
cruel God?

2. If the "prodigal son" story were called the "self-
righteous older brother" story, how would that affect my
understanding of the parable?

3. At times am I more Stoic than Christian? In what
way?

4. The Bible uses "the world" in both a positive and a
negative sense. Have I appreciated the positive sense?

5. Christians at times fear that they are "losing their faith" when in fact they are developing a more adult faith. How can one tell the difference?

6. Why is Christian Pharisaism or Christian Stoicism easier than an adult Christian faith?

For Group Discussion

1. Nicholas Lash says, "Immense human suffering has been caused by people who, lacking any profound understanding of themselves, were nevertheless quite confident that they understood God." True or false?

2. Pharisaism has an attraction for Christians because it offers security before God. Why isn't the good news enough for Christian Pharisees?

3. According to the author, religion can help angry people look very respectable. What evidence do we have to support or deny that statement?

4. When does anger stop being "just" (e.g., Jesus driving out the money-changers) and start being sinful?

5. Why do Pharisees often seem heroic?

6. In what sense are Christians sometimes responsible for the growth of atheism?

Resources

1. Nicholas Lash, *Theology on Dover Beach* (Paulist, 1979).

2. Clive S. Lewis, *The Screwtape Letters* (Macmillan, 1976).

3. Francois Varillon, *The Humility and Suffering of God* (Alba House, 1983).

5

How Can I Pray
If I'm Angry?

Frequently we speak of prayer much as we talk about love. For both we often emphasize the importance of "the mood." Certain places evoke fond memories; music and candlelight often help to create the proper atmosphere. Some times are better than others, and both pray-ers and men and women in love try to banish all "distractions" which may hinder prayer or love.

Dinner at a favorite restaurant may celebrate a couple's relationship and thus be very memorable, but is it any more *loving* than that same couple supporting one another in a hospital emergency room as they await a report on their son's car accident injuries? Is the love of a couple when they are engaged more real than their love forty years later when one of them is dying in a hospital room?

Two friends may enjoy a dinner and a movie, but is that any more loving than facing a conflict that has arisen between them? What kind of friendship places itself totally at the mercy of moods?

Although love involves moods, it goes far beyond

74

memories of loving moods. In fact, hardships enduring *together* often become the fondest memories. What do couples treasure most as they look back on fifty years of marriage? The love which was easy because the mood was favorable or the love which flowed from a *decision,* sometimes made in adverse conditions? Our experience suggests that true love is affected by moods but is not tyrannized by them.

Couples in the Marriage Encounter program describe love as a cycle of romance (Isn't she wonderful? Isn't he tremendous?), disillusionment (I never thought you would . . .), and the decision to love which faces the disillusionment but moves beyond it back to a deeper state of romance. Love, therefore, is not a goal to be achieved once-and-for-all but is the result of many decisions made by each person over the years. A love totally identified with moods can end only in disillusionment.

In recent years many people have become familiar with the idea of "tough love"—the love, for example, which challenges a family member's chemical dependency and recommends or demands entrance into treatment. Ignoring the dependency or enabling that person to hide this illness cannot be described as "loving" though the family's decision to confront the situation may not feel very loving either. Obviously "tough love" does not *feel* good, but it *is* good. Such love is not guaranteed to succeed, but it makes more sense than "peace at any price" which usually delivers a great deal of pain at a very steep price. Haven't we all seen manipulative people saying "If you really loved me, you would . . ."? Perhaps we've said that once or twice. "Tough love" sidesteps this trap.

Love has many seasons, and so does prayer. Praying when I'm happy is easy. Prayers of thanksgiving reflect an upbeat "mood." Praying when I'm confused or troubled poses no great difficulty. Although circumstances may not be the best, praying certainly seems the right thing to do. However, it may sound crazy to say that I should pray when I'm angry. Better to wait until I've "calmed down." Unfortunately, by the time many people "calm down" and feel like praying, anger has often become frozen in bitterness and the desire to pray has disappeared. Many of the psalms strike resonant chords in us precisely because the psalmist did *not* wait until "everything settled down" to start praying.

Prayer as a Decision

If the Marriage Encounter saying "Love is a decision" is true (and I believe that it is), then certainly prayer is also a decision. At times we pray while feeling that everything is fine (romance), and often we pray while feeling very distressed (disillusionment giving way to the decision to love). Either way, prayer represents a human being consciously turning to God, not a weathervane helplessly pointed as the wind (mood) determines. The distressed person who cannot pray because the "mood" is not favorable chooses, in effect, to remain in disillusionment.

In the musical *Fiddler on the Roof,* the milkman Tevye prays to God with great ease at the beginning of the story. Forced to pull his milkcart because his horse is lame, Tevye reflects on his life and sings "If I Were a Rich Man." After listing all the good things for which he would use his money, Tevye asks God, "Would it spoil some vast eternal plan if I were a wealthy man?" Tevye prays because his decision to love overcomes the disillusionment of the moment; bigger problems and more difficult prayers will soon follow. By the end of the story Tevye has seen one daughter marry a Christian and all the Jews being forced to abandon Anatevka, but he still believes that God is good.

Tevye's prayers have represented a growing decision to love.

We frequently hear of the saints spending a whole night in prayer. Perhaps many of those prayers were serene, but I suspect that often God heard some angry prayers that the saints were reluctant to express while other people were around. The story is told, for example, that St. Teresa of Avila (sixteenth-century Spanish reformer of the Carmelite Order) was once crossing a river by oxcart. When the cart tipped over, Teresa was drenched and promptly prayed, "God, if that's the way you treat your friends, it's no wonder you have so few of them." Many nights of anxious prayer about other matters may have been summarized in that one-liner.

Often prayer consoles us, but not always. Introducing the audio-cassette series *The Desert Speaks: A Journey of Prayer for the Discouraged,* Father Murray Bodo says:

> If you are like most people, you probably believe that prayer is an exaltation, an ecstasy. I believe that it is more often like a desert. This is the journey of prayer as I have experienced it and as I would share it with you, especially with you who are discouraged or desperate because of those deeper reasons that make prayer seem so hopeless right now, that brokenness or hurt that won't heal, that darkness which seems too deep for any light to penetrate. I want you to know that you are not alone.

Faith grows in many ways, including through prayers (a decision to love) made without feeling at that moment the consolations of prayer (romance). Waiting for the right "mood" means waiting for disillusionment to go away by itself. More likely, disillusionment leads to lifeless faith.

A More Fundamental Question

There's no use asking "How can I pray if I'm angry?" without asking "Why pray at any time?" Do I pray to change God's mind, to tell him things he may have forgotten? If I am waiting for a doctor's lab report, do I pray that God will change the tissue samples from malignant to benign? Or do I ask God to give me strength and friends to help me cope with whatever news the doctor reports? If I pray to change God's mind, sooner or later he is going to become a cruel God. If I pray for grace and strength, I am less likely to resent God for failing to protect me or someone else from all harm.

Knowing why I pray at all will show me what yardstick I am using to measure the success or failure of my prayer. My preferred style of prayer reflects my dominant image of God and of myself in relation to God. If those images change, my style of prayer will change also. The person who sees God as an angry Judge cannot pray in the same way as the person who sees God as a loving Creator.

If I pray to change God's mind, to tell him things he may have forgotten, then my yardstick is whether God has arranged things as I considered best. Sooner or later I will become discouraged because my praying does not seem to "get results." If I pray to change God's mind, I will be very tempted to stop praying if I think my "batting average" is poor, that is, if I've invested a lot of time and energy in prayer with very little to show for it. In Chapter 1, I mentioned that I prayed to change God's mind, to let my prematurely-born nephews live. When they died I had to ask whether God was cruel or whether I had prayed with the wrong attitude.

How do you pray when a friend or relative asks you to pray for someone who has recently suffered a heart attack? Does God need convincing to heal this person? What if you pray and the person dies? Was your prayer worthwhile? As a priest and as a member of a religious order, I am often asked to pray for this individual or that intention; sometimes the person making the request suggests that my prayers have more "pull" than their own. Each day I celebrate Mass for someone's particular intention. I've prayed for all those intentions but not with the idea that my prayers will coax a stubborn God to relent and end each story as the petitioner desires. Rather I ask God that the suffering person and his/her family will be open to God's grace, to believe that God is still good no matter what happens. I dare not pray in such a way that God has only one honorable response to my petition.

Prayer to change God's mind goes hand-in-hand with an image of God as stepping in to assure a desired outcome—for example, producing a favorable lab report. Is prayer to change God's mind a decent response to the tragedy of the swindled elderly couple, the infant born addicted to heroin or the terrorist's victims? By the time I start praying such tragedies are usually pretty far advanced—if not final. Prayer does not change *facts* although it can tremendously affect my *response* to facts.

Sooner or later, prayer to change God's mind ends up saying "If you really loved me, you would . . ." Another personal example of prayer may help here.

In Chapter 1, I mentioned that within a three-week period my father was discovered to have an inoperable malignant tumor and my mother suffered a massive stroke. Both were hospitalized for approximately two months. I prayed that Dad's cancer would go into remission (it didn't) and that Mom would recover (she did, partially and very slowly). For a time I was telling God, "If you really loved us, you would . . ." But then I saw that God was already providing our ability to deal with all this suffering. Were my prayers answered? *No* as regards remission or complete recovery of speech and movement but *yes* as regards the support of friends and family to carry on. My prayers did not change God's mind, but they did change my mind in several important ways.

Viewed in terms of supporting my parents, my sister, my three brothers and my own faith, my prayers and their prayers were certainly worthwhile. Friends and relatives who prayed also offered emotional support and various kinds of help which made all that suffering more bearable. And my parents prayed for each other. Bitterness about what might have been did not follow this double tragedy; prayer was probably the biggest factor in our responding to the situation constructively. We did what we could to ease Dad's last months and to help Mom in her recovery. For eleven years between her stroke and her death, prayer enabled Mom to be a witness in favor of God rather than one of "the devil's martyrs."

Prayers in Anger

Some of my prayers for Mom and Dad were said in anger. I know that may sound crazy to some people, but such prayers can be very genuine. The mother whose son had been killed in a one-car crash (Introduction) was ready to pray in anger because prayer seeks not to change God's mind (impossible in this case) but to speak our mind and listen closely for God's answer.

Prayer might be easier if each time God spoke to us as directly as he spoke to Moses on Mount Sinai or Paul on the road to Damascus. But God doesn't work that way in our experience. How then do we interpret God's silence?

Many of us can empathize with Lady Alice More's complaint in *A Man for All Seasons*. Imprisoned in the Tower of London for several months, More is allowed to visit with his family who urge him to take the oath that will restore him to the king's favor. More refuses but fears that without his family's support he will weaken and not follow his conscience. Lady Alice answers that she fears that when More is gone she will hate him for refusing to take the oath. More urges her to understand, embraces her and begins to cry. Lady Alice covers his mouth with her hand and says: "S-s-sh . . . As for understanding, I understand you're the best man that I ever met or am likely to; and if you go—well, God knows why, I suppose—though as God's my witness God's kept deadly quiet about it!" Prayer does not force God to break his silence but rather enables us to deal with it, to interpret it. Several angry prayers probably preceded Lady Alice's line quoted above.

Do lovers stop loving when they have a quarrel? Or do they stop loving when they stop communicating their feelings and then ignore the other's feelings? Disillusionment need not kill love, but it can if those involved refuse to make "the decision to love." Of course, a love which is terrified of a quarrel, which will not admit disillusionment, a love which is constantly "nice" and is forever keeping "peace at any price," is pretty shallow. People involved in that kind of relationship inevitably pay an extremely high price for no real peace and a great deal of tension-producing pretense.

Similarly, prayers that are forever "nice" are sooner or later dishonest. Some of the most uplifting prayers in the Bible come from men and women not afraid to voice their anger at God.

"You Have Seduced Me, Yahweh"

The prophet Jeremiah lived a long time ago (d. 568 B.C.) on the other side of the world, but his prayers have an honesty and freshness unparalleled in most of Scripture.

If Jeremiah could have chosen a different time in

which to live, he might easily have done so. When Jeremiah was about forty, Josiah, a model Jewish king, died and was followed by a king who mixed Jewish and pagan religious practices. Soon after that, the Babylonians defeated the Egyptians at Carchemish, and Jerusalem was left practically defenseless against a Babylonian takeover.

Into this maelstrom God calls Jeremiah to be a prophet. Jeremiah urges the Jewish people to repent and live out the Mosaic covenant rather than dilute that covenant with the pagan practices of their neighbors. To those who looked for Egypt to recover and save Judah from the Babylonians, Jeremiah prophesies that foreign alliances cannot save the Jewish people. His prophecies are not well received at court or anywhere else because Jeremiah criticizes the people for thinking that their worship at Solomon's temple will cover over all their sins. False prophets are flattering the people with promises of peace and prosperity. Jeremiah's enemies have imprisoned him and later thrown him into a muddy cistern. At one point Jeremiah prays boldly:

> You have seduced me, Yahweh, and I have let myself be
>   seduced;
> you have overpowered me: you were the stronger.
> I am a laughing-stock all day long,
> they all make fun of me.
> For whenever I speak, I have to howl
> and proclaim, 'Violence and ruin!'
> For me, Yahweh's word has been the cause
> of insult and derision all day long.
> I would say to myself, 'I will not think about him,
> I will not speak in his name any more,'
> but then there seemed to be a fire burning in my heart,
> imprisoned in my bones.
> The effort to restrain it wearied me,

I could not do it.
I heard so many disparaging me,
'Terror on every side!
Denounce him! Let us denounce him!'
All those who were on good terms with me
watched for my downfall.
'Perhaps he will be seduced into error.
Then we shall get the better of him
and take our revenge!'
But Yahweh is at my side like a mighty hero;
my opponents will stumble, vanquished,
confounded by their failure;
everlasting, unforgettable disgrace will be theirs.
Yahweh Sabaoth, you who test the upright,
observer of motives and thoughts,
I shall see your vengeance on them,
for I have revealed my cause to you.
Sing to Yahweh,
praise Yahweh,
for he has delivered the soul of one in need
from the clutches of evil-doers.
A curse on the day when I was born!
May the day my mother bore me be unblessed!
A curse on the man who brought my father the news,
'A son, a boy has been born to you!'
making him overjoyed.
May this man be like the towns
that Yahweh overthrew without mercy;
may he hear the warning-cry at dawn
and shout of battle at high noon,
for not killing me in the womb;
my mother would have been my grave
and her womb pregnant for ever.

Why ever did I come out of the womb
to see toil and sorrow
and end my days in shame? (20:7–18)

Now, is that a "nice" prayer? Scripture scholars tell us that in the opening line of this prayer the word Jeremiah uses— here translated as "seduced"—suggests anger and betrayal. Also, the expression "You have overpowered me" uses a word commonly linked to sexual seduction! Jeremiah is as angry a pray-er as we find in the Bible.

The passage quoted above is not a "pretty" prayer from a "nice" man. Jeremiah makes no effort to hide his anguish over the troubles which have befallen him precisely because he was faithful to his vocation as a prophet. It would be comforting to report that Jeremiah's story ended happily. In fact, Jerusalem was captured by the Babylonians in 587 B.C., Solomon's temple was razed, and the leading citizens of Judah were taken off to Babylon. The destruction of Jerusalem was even more devastating for the Jewish people than the attack on Pearl Harbor was for the Americans in 1941. We are not sure what happened to Jeremiah, but according to one tradition he was carried off to Egypt by a group of Jewish exiles and later murdered there. In another sense, however, Jeremiah's story ended happily, for he persevered as God's prophet, and his words and actions have nourished the faith of later believers.

What Good Do Prayers in Anger Do?

Do you consider Jeremiah's prayer a success or a failure? If we measure it with the yardstick of change-God's-mind-to-assure-a-desired-outcome, then Jeremiah was a dismal failure. If we use the yardstick of speak-your-mind-to-God-and-accept-the-grace-to-live-with-what-happens, then Jeremiah's prayer was very successful.

Praying while I am angry can accomplish two vital tasks. I can see myself without my public image, what I would like others to believe is the real me. The more honest I am with myself, the more likely I'll be honest with God and others. But equally important, prayers in anger can help me see more sharply the God to whom I pray. Prayers in anger have helped many people to discard faulty notions of God and grow in faith. If Job had not prayed in anger, he might never have left behind the deuteronomic theology so dear to his friends.

Prayer in anger undoubtedly helped Jeremiah decide whether he would sell out and become one of the "good times" prophets—better pay and less hassle—or whether he would continue announcing God's word despite the hardships. If Jeremiah had not prayed in anger, if he had "calmed down" before he prayed, his career as a prophet might have been stillborn in the anger of resentment.

Uncensored Prayer

If in prayer I give voice to what is in my heart, then my prayer is genuine. If I separate my feelings into "nice" and "not nice" and then use only "nice" feelings in prayer, I attempt to pray a lie. The reason that Jeremiah's prayer strikes us as authentic is that he did not censor his feelings *or* his prayer.

Especially in grief people are tempted to censor their feelings and their prayer. How can I pray if I tell myself "I shouldn't feel this way"? The fact is, I *do* feel this way, and denying that fact undermines all my prayer. Sometimes the grieving person is ready to pray in anger, but someone else—like one of Job's friends—suggests: "You shouldn't feel that way." Fine, now the grieving person has to contend with grief plus the guilt for feeling that way. If I say "You shouldn't feel that way," what I am really saying is "I don't know how to deal with the *fact* that you feel the way you do—so I'll try to shame you into not feeling that way."

It's bad enough if I censor my own prayers, but trying to censor someone else's is even worse. Dispirited belief, agnosticism or atheism may result. What kind of a God is so fragile that he must be protected from honest expressions of human emotion? Is any God so fragile worth believing in?

Unresolved Anger:
The Number One Killer of
Our Life With God

If I cannot pray in anger, I am headed either toward atheism or toward a lifeless faith. Censoring the feelings I bring to prayer means that my prayers reflect less and less of the most important concerns of my life at that moment; it's like trying to talk to one person at a party while always looking around the room at the other guests, the refreshments or the furniture.

Because atheism strikes many people as a too-radical solution for their anger at God, Jews and Christians may prefer to remain believers in name but think of God as more and more aloof, more and more attentive to cosmic issues and less concerned about the joys and sufferings of individual people.

In the confessional and in ordinary conversation, I have met men and women beaten down by their unresolved anger at God. Frequently they could admit that they were angry at this or that person, but such an admission failed to deal with the root problem: their inability to admit anger at God. Though they might complain of difficulties in prayer or say that their lives lacked overall purpose or meaning, they kept the more basic issue at arm's length. Time had not healed their wounds, and yet they were reluctant to face their anger and the incidents which sparked it. It was as though they preferred to live with a splinter rather than endure the pain caused by removing it. Sometimes fearful of losing their faith, these men and women can cling to a faith which is increasingly oppressive because it makes sense only if God is aloof and cruel. I consider unresolved anger at God the number one killer of our life with God.

On the other hand, in the confessional and in ordinary conversation I have met women and men who could face their anger at God. Lightning did not strike them when they admitted such anger. That admission did not remove all problems, but at least the person could address the issue more openly and wrestle with the accompanying conflicting feelings.

Prayer as Wrestling with God

Honest prayer can be a very exhausting experience. For nine years I lived in a friary with a unique work of art on the chapel tabernacle. This copper and enamel piece depicted Jacob wrestling with God (Gn 32:23–33). Jacob wrestled all night with an unidentified adversary. The adversary told Jacob that henceforth his name would be Israel "since you have shown your strength against God and men and have prevailed" (v. 29). Later Jacob realized that he had seen God face to face.

When I first came to that friary, I considered this a strange biblical scene to put on the front of a tabernacle. But the longer I prayed before that tabernacle, the more this scene seemed appropriate. In prayer we wrestle with many opposing feelings, and yet precisely in that struggle we see God more clearly. If I have to be in the right mood and have only "nice" thoughts before I can pray, I have excluded a sizable portion of my life from prayer.

Did Job's friends ever wrestle with God in prayer?

Probably not. Their theology, and more importantly their compassion, suffered as a result.

Prayers expressed in anger have led many people to conclude that God's love and his justice require a life beyond this one, a life where his values reign supreme and the prosperity of evil-doers is shown to be short-lived. The next chapter will focus on the growth of that belief throughout God's revelation.

For Personal Reflection

1. How do my moods affect my prayer? Do I ever find prayer impossible because of my mood?

2. Can I pray while angry? Would I be better off waiting until I've "cooled down"?

3. What am I agreeing to do when I say I'll pray for a sick friend or relative? Does my prayer encourage acts of charity on behalf of the person(s) for whom I have prayed?

4. What has been the biggest crisis of my prayer life? How did it influence my image of God?

5. Is unresolved anger at God the real cause of my continuing anger with certain people?

6. Has my prayer ever been a wrestling with God?

For Group Discussion

1. How many people talk to God with the easy manner which Tevye used? What helps such frankness?

2. In what way is prayer a "desert experience"?

3. How does a person's image of God influence the way he/she prays and sees himself/herself?

4. We often speak of God as being silent while we pray. How does God answer our prayers even if things do not turn out as we had hoped?

5. Why would "nice" people be better off if they could pray in anger as well as in joy or petition?

6. We frequently talk of the saints as though they never prayed in anger. Are there any incidents which suggest the contrary?

Resources

1. Murray Bodo, O.F.M. and Susan Saint Sing, *The Desert Speaks: A Journey of Prayer for the Discouraged,* an audio-cassette series from St. Anthony Messenger Press, 1984.

2. Robert Bolt, *A Man for All Seasons* (Random House, 1962).

3. John Sanford, *The Man Who Wrestled With God: Light from the Old Testament on the Psychology of Individuation* (Paulist, 1981). The chapters on Isaac, Joseph and Moses show how each one grew in prayer as his understanding of God expanded.

4. William A. Miller, *Make Friends with Your Shadow: How To Accept and Use the Negative Side of Your Personality* (Augsburg, 1981).

5. Matthew and Dennis Linn, S.J., *Healing of Memories* (Paulist, 1974). The authors have developed this subject in later books and tapes.

6. Thomas Green, S.J., *When the Well Runs Dry: Prayer Beyond the Beginnings* (Ave Maria, 1979).

7. Basil Cardinal Hume, *To Be a Pilgrim: A Spiritual Notebook* (Harper and Row, 1984).

8. Bishop Desmond Tutu, *Hope and Suffering: Sermons and Speeches* (Eerdmans, 1984).

6

The Afterlife:
Vindicating God's Values

Believing that there is a life beyond this one can be controversial. Over the centuries critics have said that such a belief represents wishful thinking at best and spineless escapism at worst. Is believing in an afterlife really "copping out"—not taking the present seriously enough because one's attention is too much on the future?

I understand these criticisms because people can use belief in an afterlife as an excuse for shirking present responsibilities, of looking the other way at injustices because "God will make it all up in heaven." Quietism, one name for this particular form of blindness, considers God's intention (what he would like to happen) as inevitable; such a theology appeals to those enjoying prosperity (Job's friends) but has nothing to say to suffering men and women. Quietism almost obliterates human freedom and personal responsibility. Waiting for God to step in and shape up his creation represents the highest wisdom. Perhaps those condemned at the final judgment for neglecting the hungry and the naked (Mt 25) felt that such acts of charity were wasted because God straightens everything out in eternity anyway. Besides, didn't Jesus say, "You have the poor with you always" (Jn 12:8)?

Believing in an afterlife understandably has a bad reputation among some people. It can lead to an unhealthy passivity—religion as the "opiate of the people," to use Marx's expression. According to an old I.W.W. song, "There'll be pie in the sky when you die."

While granting that there has been some cause for the above complaints, we should also remember that people who deny any afterlife are not necessarily generous and civic-minded. They include ruthless hedonists of the "Eat, drink and be merry for tomorrow we die" variety. Those who deny the afterlife do not all fall into one group, nor do those who affirm the afterlife. Abuses are possible on each side.

In this chapter I will try to explain why believing in an afterlife can help people deal with their anger at God and at life's injustices. Naturally, I cannot speak for everyone who believes in an afterlife. My ideas on this subject reflect my Roman Catholic background and its view of God's world; however, I know that my explanation harmonizes with what many other Christians believe. These ideas are also strongly influenced by Christianity's Jewish roots, especially the Judaism of the last two hundred years before Christ. Some Jewish people continue to believe strongly in an afterlife.

Does Christian belief in an afterlife foster poor citizens and irresponsible neighbors in this life. If Christians sometimes shirk their civic and humanitarian responsibilities, doesn't the explanation for that lie in not allowing the good news to permeate their entire lives? If Christians live up to their name, they will respect the world which God the Father has created and in which God the Son became incarnate so that all of us could be saved. The world around us contains "God's footprints." God uses it to reveal himself. Other people are not simply hindrances to my individual salvation, as Christian Stoicism would have us believe. In the Book of Genesis, the first account of creation ends, "God saw all he had made, and indeed it was very good" (Gn 1:31). Has sin entirely spoiled God's creation?

Clive Staples Lewis (d. 1963), a literature professor, popular novelist and an extraordinarily perceptive theologian, once wrote:

> Hope is one of the theological virtues. This means that a continual looking to the eternal world is not (as some modern people think) a form of escapism or wishful thinking, but one of the things a Christian is meant to do. It does not mean that we are to leave the present world as it is. If you read history you will find that the Christians who did the most for the present world were just those who thought most of the next. The Apostles themselves, who set on foot the conversion of the Roman Empire, the great men who built up the Middle Ages, the English Evangelicals who abolished the Slave Trade, all left their mark on Earth, precisely because their minds were occupied with Heaven. It is since Christians have largely ceased to think of the other world that they have become so ineffective in this. Aim at Heaven and you will get Earth "thrown in": aim at Earth and you will get neither. (*Mere Christianity*)

I believe that Lewis is correct. Wherever Christians are good citizens, that fact should be largely credited to their belief in a life beyond this one, a life where God's goodness ultimately triumphs and where sacrifices once thought foolish are seen as wise. By being good citizens here and accepting the importance of the present moment (without denying the importance of the past and the future),

Christians promote the values which will be perfected and made permanent in God's kingdom which has already begun.

In Vatican II's *Pastoral Constitution on the Church in the Modern World,* the bishops address this issue when they teach:

> The Council exhorts Christians, as citizens of both cities, to perform their duties faithfully in the spirit of the Gospel. It is a mistake to think that, because we have here no lasting city, but seek the city which is to come (Heb 13:14), we are entitled to shirk our earthly responsibilities; this is to forget that by our faith we are bound all the more to fulfill these responsibilities according to the vocation of each one. But it is no less mistaken to think that we may immerse ourselves in earthly activities as if these latter were nothing more than the fulfillment of acts of worship and the observance of a few moral obligations. . . . The Christian who shirks his temporal duties shirks his duties toward his neighbor, neglects God himself, and endangers his eternal salvation. (§43)

Later in the same document the bishops add:

> In their pilgrimage to the heavenly city, Christians are to seek and relish the things that are above (Col 3:1–2): this involves not a lesser, but a greater commitment to working with all men toward the establishment of a world that is more human. Indeed, the mystery of the Christian faith provides them with an outstanding incentive and encouragement to fulfill their role even more eagerly and to discover the full sense of the commitment by which human culture becomes important in man's total vocation. (§57)

Not all Catholics have seen or now see their responsibility to this world in the terms described above. But repenting and accepting the good news has very immediate and practical consequences, as John the Baptist told the tax collectors, soldiers and those with an extra coat (Lk 3:10–14). Perhaps it is easier to live exclusively for the present or for the future, but Jesus has announced a kingdom linking both time-frames, a kingdom which has already begun but is not yet complete.

My Disagreement with Rabbi Kushner

Before presenting part of the biblical evidence for a life beyond this one, I would like to challenge Rabbi Kushner's statement, "The dead depend on us for their redemption and their immortality." It is true, as Kushner says, that the living make the dead into witnesses for or against God. Because we give suffering a positive or negative meaning, we can turn the person who died into one of "the devil's martyrs."

Kushner's book suggests that in some way his son's life has been redeemed by the family's growth in compassion and by the author's decision to share his story, thereby explaining the blind alleys and through streets he encountered in dealing with this suffering. True. He also says that he would trade all of that in an instant if doing so could bring back his son. Rabbi Kushner's book and his speeches have inspired millions of people, including me.

But is it fair to suggest that the meaning of one person's life is entirely dependent on how that person's survivors deal with their grief? What shall we say of a child who dies of progeria (Aaron's Kushner's disease) and one of the parents suffers a nervous breakdown from which he/she never recovers? Is the dead child denied redemption because this tragedy has caused one of the parents to become, in the minds of some people, a witness against God? Is memory the only immortality? What of the murdered child? The divorce rate among parents of murdered children is very high because the memories of that child are often overwhelmingly painful. What redemption is there for the "marginal" people in any society? For the young man or woman who runs away to the big city, drifts into prostitution and is murdered at nineteen, unclaimed in the city morgue? What redemption is there for the more than fifteen thousand people drowned in the Bay of Bengal by a tidal wave one day in May of 1985? Are there enough survivors to redeem each one as Kushner's book has redeemed his son? In two hundred years will the holocaust be sufficiently remembered to redeem the lives of the millions who died in Nazi concentration camps? Does Josef Mengele, the "Angel of Death" at Auschwitz, never have to answer for his crimes?

Each man, woman and child is too valuable to have his/her worth inexorably linked to the survivors' ability to bring some good out of a tragedy. If a surviving parent should crack under the strain of a child's "crib death" and then commit suicide, that is doubly tragic, but can that be allowed to rob the dead child of his/her worth?

True, in some sense the living redeem the dead. College scholarships, university libraries and hospital wings are often established in memory of a deceased friend or relative. Additional examples will be cited in Chapter 7. But in another sense, the dead have an intrinsic worth which makes redemption by remembrance a bonus but not a necessity.

To be fair to Rabbi Kushner, I must admit that he does not vehemently deny the possibility of an afterlife; he has not yet found enough evidence in favor of it. Also, he fears that believing in an afterlife engenders an unhealthy passiv-

ity about the sufferings of this life. I can empathize with
some of the difficulties he cites, but ultimately I cannot
accept the idea that God's values, God's justice and mercy
will never be permanently established anywhere but rather
are established only where women and men can redeem the
dead through memory. Such redemption requires sufficient
leisure and enough thinking and verbal skills to deal with
wrenching feelings of loss and eventually see the deceased
person as a witness in favor of God and not against him. I
commend Rabbi Kushner for the sense in which he has
redeemed his son's death, but I also support the men,
women and children who believe that a good God does not
rely totally on human effort to vindicate his ways against
people who consider God's values foolish and worthless.

The Book of Wisdom and Eternal Life

"The souls of the upright are in the hands of God, and
no torment can touch them," says the Book of Wisdom
(3:1). That bold assurance revolutionized the Hebrew
Scriptures, for most of those books were written by people
who did not believe in an afterlife (Chapter 2). How and
why Judaism developed a belief in the afterlife is a story
worth telling.

In the years after the Jewish nation's return from cap-
tivity in Babylon (539 B.C.), the Jewish people became
more interior and individualistic in a good sense. The idea
of individual responsibility grows and supports the belief in
personal immortality. Indeed, God rejects the proverb,
"The parents have eaten unripe grapes; and the children's
teeth are set on edge," but rather proclaims, "The one who
has sinned is the one to die" (Ez 18:2, 4). God knows and
loves individual women, men and children—not simply
masses of people.

When Jerusalem was destroyed by the Babylonians, many Jewish people moved to Asia Minor and Egypt where they were a minority. Two centuries later the entire Mediterranean basin came under Greek influence. Then Alexander the Great established the largest empire the western world had ever known. A key part of his strategy for uniting diverse peoples was Hellenization, the mixing of Greek culture and the local cultures throughout the empire. Thus eventually we find Greek temples and stadiums throughout the Near East, and Syrian and Egyptian goddesses start to be worshiped in Greece. Hellenization thrived on syncretism, a "melting pot" approach to architecture, food, clothing, business customs, athletics, language and religion. People who believe in many gods may find syncretism attractive, but for monotheists like the Jews, such a belief is corporate suicide.

In time some Jews were completely Hellenized and became pagans. Thus many other Jewish people feared being swallowed up by Hellenization and so resisted it wherever possible. A third group within Judaism felt that they could learn Greek and adopt a few Hellenistic customs without sacrificing their Jewish identity. It was among Egyptian Jews in this third category that the Book of Wisdom originated, perhaps as late as 50 B.C.

Because this book was originally written in Greek, not all the Jews accepted it as inspired; Rabbi Kushner apparently shares that opinion. However, many Jews before the birth of Christ and the earliest Jewish Christians accepted this book as inspired. Thus Catholic and Protestant Bibles differ in the Hebrew Scriptures. Protestant Bibles are shorter because they and most Jews today accept only the books originally written in Hebrew. Bibles used by the Roman Catholic and Orthodox churches include seven additional books originally written in Greek.

The Book of Wisdom was written to strengthen the faith of Jews seeking answers to questions such as: What is unique about Judaism? How is it that wicked and godless people so often prosper while just men and women suffer? Is Judaism deficient in wisdom, the goal of Hellenistic life?

The Book of Wisdom represents a quantum leap in Jewish theology; personal immortality is affirmed even if bodily resurrection is not. Jews need not envy pagan wisdom, for their Scriptures represent a true wisdom, gained in part by individual hard work (attentiveness and discipline) but ultimately a gift from God. In effect, this book says: Let the pagans follow their fatalism to its dead end; the God of Abraham, Isaac and Jacob rules over all creation (the living and the dead).

Immortality, the Reward of Wisdom

This subhead rather accurately describes the first section of the Book of Wisdom which begins with an exhortation to love justice and live justly. After demonstrating how the godless think and why they envy the upright, the author says:

> Death came into the world only through the Devil's envy,
> as those who belong to him find to their cost. (2:24)

Then the author immediately counters:

> But the souls of the upright are in the hands of God,
> and no torment can touch them.
> To the unenlightened, they appeared to die,
> their departure was regarded as a disaster,
> their leaving us like an annihilation;
> but they are at peace.

If, as it seemed to us, they suffered punishment,
their hope was rich with immortality;
slight was their correction, great will their blessings be.
God was putting them to the test
and has proved them worthy to be with him;
he has tested them like gold in a furnace,
and accepted them as a perfect burnt offering.
At their time of visitation, they will shine out;
as sparks run through the stubble, so will they.
They will judge nations, rule over peoples,
and the Lord will be their king for ever.
Those who trust in him will understand the truth,
those who are faithful will live with him in love;
for grace and mercy await his holy ones,
and he intervenes on behalf of his chosen. (3:1–9)

The writer then offers counsels about God's providence even for those who die childless or at an early age.

The remainder of the Book of Wisdom encourages its readers to seek genuine wisdom and offers a review of God's providence in bringing the Israelites out of Egypt. This book is not the only affirmation of an afterlife in the Hebrew Scriptures (2 Mac 7 and 12:38–46, written about the same time as the Book of Wisdom), but it clearly moves beyond the idea that immortality is only through remembrance among the living.

The Book of Wisdom strongly influences the New Testament. The key Gospel term "reign of God" occurs in Wisdom 10:10 but nowhere else in the Hebrew Scriptures. The New Testament quotes generously from the Book of Wisdom which even appears as a New Testament writing in one ancient collection! This book certainly offers a bridge between the Hebrew Scriptures and the New Testament, supporting the *anawim* theology we find in Luke (especially chapters 1–2) and in the Sermon on the Mount.

A Sampling of New Testament Evidence on Personal Immortality

Presently some Christians are becoming more unsure about the afterlife. The New Testament, however, makes no sense if we rule out a life beyond this one. Jesus would be reduced to the level of a moral philosopher like Socrates or Confucius. Denying the afterlife guts the Gospels and robs Jesus' preaching of its unique power. The Beatitudes become "lofty ideals," not a description of discipleship. The parables of readiness (servants and the talents, ten bridesmaids, etc.) become quaint stories, and the story of Lazarus and the rich man (Lk 16:19–31) is allegorized into oblivion. What can we make of the Gospel stories about the last becoming first and vice versa (e.g., the Pharisee and the tax collector praying in the temple, Lk 18:9–14)? If there is no afterlife, where does the reversal take place? If there is no afterlife, what does Jesus' resurrection mean?

Denying any afterlife reinterprets the entire New Testament. As Paul told the Christians in Corinth, "If Christ has not been raised, your faith is pointless and you have not, after all, been released from your sins. In addition, those who have fallen asleep in Christ are utterly lost. If our hope in Christ has been for this life only, we are of all people the most pitiable" (1 Cor 15:17–19). Denying an afterlife turns the Letter to the Hebrews, the Book of Revelation and the Catholic epistles into gibberish.

The Other Side of the Coin

For Christians, believing in an afterlife means that ultimately we will live with God (heaven) or apart from God (hell). Though it may seem generous to say that God will not let a single person perish forever, that answer raises more problems than it solves. God *wants* each man, woman and child to be saved, but God does not make the opposite outcome impossible. Otherwise, human freedom becomes radically insignificant, the Gospel call to repent becomes optional, and any talk about a final judgment must be banished. Fear of hell cannot make men and women into faithful followers of Jesus or good neighbors in this world. But believing in heaven while denying the possibility of hell means taking a scissors-and-paste approach to the New Testament, leaving much of it in the garbage can.

Details Unimportant

It's one thing to say there is an afterlife; it's quite another to describe the details of such a life. Because the Gospels offer images but few details, our most common images about heaven and hell arise from popular imagination. The Scriptures do not say, for example, that everyone in heaven wears a long white robe and plays a harp. They do not say that the devil has horns, a tail and a pitchfork. One can suspend judgment on many details of the afterlife without denying it altogether.

In Conclusion

If some people are satisfied with believing that God's goodness does not require an afterlife, so be it. But many people cannot understand how God can be all-good if there is no afterlife. Somewhere God's values must reign supreme because they will never be completely vindicated here on earth. If there is no afterlife, many Christians will reluctantly have to join Verdi's Iago in proclaiming "I believe in a cruel God."

Those who deny any afterlife may double their efforts to be good citizens, to promote the common good and alleviate human suffering. But all too often they become discouraged at the huge imbalance between others' needs and their ability to address them. "Burnout" frequently sets in and people often retreat to a smaller world of needs where their efforts bring more immediate and gratifying results. On the other hand, men and women who believe in an afterlife may see the same human needs, work with great zeal in addressing them and yet not give in to discouragement because their small efforts are a foretaste of heaven where every tear will be wiped away and God will be enough for everyone.

Only an afterlife can fully redeem the victims of man-made evil and those who suffer from the forces of nature. Other avenues (e.g., loving memory) may partially redeem some people, but those solutions raise as many questions as they answer.

We can still be good citizens, good neighbors, and fulfill our present responsibilities even if we believe in an afterlife. Indeed, as Chesterton said, "The moment we have a fixed heart we have a free hand" (*Orthodoxy*). Believing in an afterlife can strengthen our resolve to promote justice in this life as we await the consolation of seeing God and our loved ones face to face. Believing in an afterlife can build up a compassionate community (Chapter 7) rather than weaken it.

For Personal Reflection

1. Have I seen Christians whose belief in an afterlife seemed to foster irresponsibility toward present duties?

2. Does the good news permeate my life enough to help me be a good citizen? What conclusion do I draw from Jesus' statement "You have the poor with you always" (Jn 12:8)?

3. In what sense is "the world" an aid to my life with God? A hindrance?

4. Whose life has been for me the strongest evidence in favor of God? The strongest argument against God? Why?

5. If fear of hell doesn't make good Christians or good neighbors, what does?

6. What do I think of Chesterton's saying "The moment we have a fixed heart we have a free hand"?

For Group Discussion

1. Have you ever seen belief in heaven promoting an unhealthy passivity about other people's suffering?
2. Have you ever seen belief in an afterlife promoting greater concern for the "common good"?
3. If every person is valuable in God's sight, doesn't that fact require a life beyond this one?
4. What happens to one's reading of the New Testament if personal immortality is denied?
5. Why do we sometimes like to speculate about the details of heaven and hell where the Scriptures are silent?
6. Does believing in an afterlife help you deal with feelings of "burnout"?

Resources

1. C.S. Lewis, *Mere Christianity* (Macmillan, 1952).

2. Gilbert Keith Chesterton, *Orthodoxy* (Doubleday, 1973).

3. C.S. Lewis, *The Great Divorce* (Macmillan, 1978). The inhabitants of hell go on a bus tour of heaven. The conversations they have with various people in heaven are humorous and full of insight.

7

Community: Gateway to Bitterness or Compassion

Although all animals experience pain, only human beings try to find meaning in suffering. Even though all animals know physical pain, only men, women and children can know the unique pain caused by a personal failure or rejection by a loved one. And most importantly, only human beings can decide how suffering will affect a person's future.

At some point, people in pain usually seek the help of others. Depending on the help received, suffering people become either more or less compassionate. Rabbi Kushner says that Job's friends made a serious mistake when they gave a theological answer to Job's anguished question, "Why is God doing this to me?" Job needed compassion, not their smug theology. He needed to hear that he is still a good person and not the target of God's special punishment. He needed to know that others feel his pain and can keep quiet as he vents his anger—in short, he needed what his friends did *not* offer: a compassionate community.

Rabbi Kushner says that for all their mistakes Job's friends did two things right: they came and they listened. According to the biblical story, they sat in silence for seven days as Job poured out his grief and anger. If only they had listened from the heart to Job's anguish and reconsidered the "comfort" they were about to offer!

A Fork in the Road

People in great pain stand at a fork in life's road. One path leads to increased bitterness, selfishness and greater withdrawal from solidarity with others. The other path eventually leads to compassion, generosity and a greater unity with the rest of the human family. Naturally the person in great pain does not see bright neon signs or huge billboards describing where each path leads. Genuine friends help the suffering person choose the road which leads to a more human life. True friends will walk with a person in pain. Shallow friends are usually embarrassed by someone else's pain and often urge the person to deny it; if that strategy fails, such friends tend to avoid the suffering person.

When people in a community (family, friends, a religious group, a social club) are at their best, they give us time and space to express our feelings honestly. Then they work with us as we decide what to do about our feelings, for there are always choices to be made. No single course of action is inevitable. Since my pain is excruciating when I know there is nothing I can do to reverse some tragedy (for example, another person's cancer or a stroke), I may be tempted to think that the last shred of my humanity has been stripped away. Members of a community will show me—more by deeds than by words—that my ability to choose is my last shred of humanity. I may surrender that unique human characteristic, but no one steals it from me.

When members of a community are at their worst, they refuse to deal with our feelings of pain and sorrow.

They frequently urge us to "snap out of it" and rejoin a camaraderie which will be shallow as long as it fears honesty. In effect, that approach urges us to become bitter and withdrawn—which is exactly what Job would have become if he had accepted the advice of his three friends.

Compassion: A More Sensible Response

God does not make us suffer in the hope that we will become more compassionate men and women. If he did, his "batting average" would be rather mediocre, and he would indeed be a cruel God. But given the *fact* of innocent human suffering, compassion is a more sensible *response* than any other option. When the suffering is caused by someone's *abuse* of human freedom (as opposed to suffering caused by "acts of God"), the need for compassion is even more acute. Rebuilding one's life after a tornado is generally easier than rebuilding it after a lifelong friend has been killed by a hit-and-run driver.

Don't the greatest works of charity usually come from women and men who have suffered themselves and have decided not to become "the devil's martyrs" (witnesses against God and the meaningfulness of a moral life)? Day after day such men and women have taken the other fork in the road, and that has made all the difference in their lives.

It's easy to imagine, for example, that in the Good Samaritan story (Lk 10:25–37) the Samaritan was rich (he gave the innkeeper an unlimited budget, didn't he?), not in a hurry to do something else (unlike the priest and the levite), and unconcerned about his own safety (the man in need was beaten by robbers who might still be around). Our experience, however, suggests that the Good Samaritan was compassionate precisely because he had suffered himself and because he had chosen to meet that suffering with increased solidarity. The priest and levite had probably suffered too, but apparently they reacted with lessened solidarity. They hardened their hearts and took the other fork in the road—that day and probably in the future.

Anger (even at God) can sometimes lead people to compassion. In 1980, Cari Lightner was killed by a drunk driver. Her mother Candy started MADD (Mothers Against Drunk Driving) and began a one-woman campaign to change the drunk driving laws in her state, California. She did and her organization became nationwide and has inspired spinoffs such as SADD (Students Against Drunk Driving). Five years after Candy Lightner started MADD, it counted 360 local chapters and 600,000 members. None of this will bring Cari Lightner or anyone else killed by a drunk driver back to life, but perhaps it can prevent that tragedy from becoming more common. In any case, MADD is a clear example of anger ending in compassion.

In 1978, Richard King, a radio disc jockey in Cincinnati, and his wife started the Ricky King Fund in honor of their four-year-old son, Ricky, who died from Reye's Syndrome. Money raised through dances, long-distance runs, corporate contributions and private donations helps Children's Hospital Medical Center in Cincinnati continue its research into Reye's Syndrome and other fatal or crippling children's diseases. This fund will not bring Ricky King back to life, but it helps keep him from being one of "the devil's martyrs."

In 1980, Terry Fox, a young man with bone cancer and an artificial leg, began walking across Canada in order to raise money for cancer research. Terry completed more than half the walk before health problems forced him to stop—but not before he had raised more than $20,000,000 for research and gained the attention and admiration of the world. That walk also inspired others suffering from bone cancer. In May 1985, Steve Fonyo, a nineteen-year-old man with bone cancer and an artificial leg, completed a fourteen-month, 4,924 mile walk from St. Johns, Newfoundland to Victoria, British Columbia. By the walk's end, Fonyo had raised nearly ten million dollars, with contributions still coming in. Both men raised the world's consciousness about the need for more cancer research and better treatment methods. These walks did not decrease their sufferings, but they gave these men new purpose and brought thousands of people to a new level of awareness and compassion.

You probably know several stories similar to these four. Many charitable organizations began in memory of individuals who had suffered greatly. These groups continue to grow because others who have suffered see them as constructive outlets for their pain and grief. When a friend or relative dies, memorials to such organizations are often suggested.

Other Responses

Another increasingly common way in which suffering men and women turn their anger into compassion is through support groups which break down the sense of isolation ("I'm the only one who ever experienced this") and offer the example of other people who have suffered the same loss and yet are coping with it. Alcoholics Anonymous is perhaps the oldest such group, and there every member knows that sobriety is a day-by-day decision. Depending on where you live, there may be a few, dozens or hundreds of support groups serving, for example, parents of children who died from Sudden Infant Death Syndrome, families dealing with a member's drug dependency, battered women, teens dealing with adjustments arising from divorce, widows, widowers, women recovering from a mastectomy, unemployed men and women, colostomy patients, heart attack victims, diabetics—the potential is almost unlimited.

Sometimes the suffering person may not join a group tailored to his/her need but will keep in contact with one fellow sufferer willing to retell his/her story and ready to encourage the newly-suffering person. For example, more and more doctors are putting current patients in contact with former patients who suffered the same loss.

How many shelters are there for teens who have run away from their families? How many "hotlines" are there for people contemplating suicide or otherwise in urgent need of someone to listen? Constructive responses to suffering begin whenever people are willing to step out and share their pain and hear how others have decided to carry on—not denying the pain but not being tyrannized by it either.

Various kinds of fundraisers (e.g., bowling for cystic fibrosis, long-distance runs to promote the fight against heart disease, special collections in churches, the Live Aid concert to fight famine in Africa) depend on some level of anger which can be channeled toward a positive result. When people decide they can no longer cope with suffering (their own or someone else's) as they did before, they move either toward despair or toward some better way of coping. When communities are at their best, they show suffering men, women and children that their suffering matters and that they need not bear it all alone. "Attention must be paid," says Willie Loman's wife about her husband's sufferings (*Death of a Salesman*).

Failing To "Pay Attention"

For all their potential to help suffering women and men deal with intense personal suffering, communities often miss those opportunities or use them inadequately. Although there are various reasons why other communities fail, when people in the Christian community fail, their individual and collective image of God and of other people is often the major factor.

For example, is anyone surprised that Pharisees (Jewish, Christian and their non-religious counterparts) tend to lack compassion? By definition, Pharisees are an elite group. Not everyone has the insight, they think, to understand all the rules God considers important and even fewer people possess the courage to observe all those rules. Because they remake God in their own image, Pharisees cannot take seriously the sufferings of non-Pharisees. True, almsgiving is recommended but self-interest makes other-centered service impossible. Should any Pharisees suffer and complain, that proves they weren't very good Pharisees in the first place; besides, they probably weren't observing all the laws anyway. In the hands of Pharisees, loving God can become a noble excuse for ignoring the needs of others.

Similarly, the Stoic understanding of God makes compassion extremely difficult if not impossible. In the *Peanuts* cartoon strip. Linus once said, "I love mankind. It's people I can't stand." No Stoic could have said it better. The abstract "mankind" can always be kept at a safe distance; addressing the sufferings of Heather or Brian threatens my always-precarious self-sufficiency. If I get involved, I could get hurt. In the words of a Simon and Garfunkel song, "If I never loved, I never would have cried. I am a rock; I am an island." Better to play it "cool." If I look at God through Stoic eyes, inevitably I see other people through the same eyes. However much Stoics may rhapsodize about the human family, they cannot form a compassionate community because "compassion" means "to suffer with" someone, and the Stoics have identified that as a vice, not a virtue.

Jesus tells us that there are two great commandments: loving God with all our strength and loving our neighbor as ourselves (Lk 10:27). In different ways, Christian Pharisees and Stoic Christians think they can follow the first commandment while ignoring the second. Never mind that Jesus preaches and lives out both commandments, that the Letter of James carefully raises and denies the possibility (2:14–25), and that the First Letter of John clearly tells us, "Whoever does not love the brother whom he can see cannot love God whom he has not seen" (4:20).

Already in the sixth century, Gregory the Great explained that Jesus sent the disciples two by two to preach because the commands of love are twofold: love God and love your neighbor. A compassionate community cannot take away anyone's suffering, but through example, acts of charity and prayer it can help the person deal with that suffering more effectively.

In a sense, Pharisaism and Stoicism are easier than Christian love of God and neighbor because the Pharisee and the Stoic begin with a total understanding of God and all creation. No need to repent, no need to grow—only to protect that understanding from any pollution. Disciples, on the other hand, must continually repent and constantly see new depths to the two great commandments. Our understanding of God gives direction to our prayer. Likewise, common prayer gives new direction to our love of God and neighbor.

Common Prayer: Bridging the Gap

For people who believe in God, common prayer represents an important way through which they become and remain more compassionate people. Such prayer can influence which fork in the road sufferers take because it helps suffering men and women to see that the community is strong enough to share their most joyous and most frightening experiences. Suffering does not have to be faced alone.

In this regard Rabbi Kushner explains three prayerful Jewish customs. When someone dies, for a week afterward, friends and relatives come to the person's home for *shiva,* to sit with the grieving family, listen to their stories and remind them that they are still part of a community—even when their first impulse may be to do all their mourning in private. The living grieve and yet go on living. For the second custom, the meal of replenishment, when the mourners return from the cemetery, they are not to fix food for themselves or for others but are to eat food prepared by someone else as a reminder of the community's solidarity with them. And, finally, a mourning relative recites the Mourner's Kaddish in the synagogue for a year after the person's death. The Kaddish affirms that God is still good and that he has made a good world. Those who recite the Kaddish see and hear other mourners and know the support of the larger community.

Common prayer (Jewish, Catholic, Baptist, or of whatever denomination) links us to a network, a community of faith, of people who care what happens to us, who care whether our grief ends in despair or in greater hope.

In common prayer we do not lose our grief but rather see it in a different context. In common worship, those who do not feel any particular grief or void can come to the aid of those who do. Common worship can stretch our horizons and nurture greater compassion. Naturally, such prayer is not guaranteed to do this every time, but it does have that potential.

For those who believe in a life beyond this one, common prayer powerfully denies that death has the last word.

In the Eucharist, for example, Catholics pray to God with all the holy women and men back to Adam and Eve. They pray for those present and are united with the Church throughout the world; they pray for all those who have died. The word of God, with its power to console and its power to confront, is heard in common; all who receive the Eucharist share a common bond. Since the community acknowledges and prays for the needs of the whole Church, the Eucharist has a tremendous potential for relinking its participants to the death and resurrection of Jesus and to one another.

Why Common Prayer Sometimes Fails

But if community can be a gateway to bitterness or to compassion, its common prayer at times fails to promote solidarity and compassion. One obvious reason is that people may look for the community's compassion yet not join in such prayer. Communal pray-ers can complain about those not coming, but men and women worshiping together should occasionally ask themselves if they have played the part of Job's friends—urging others to deny their pain or to assume guilt they do not deserve. It's hard to imagine that Job could pray with his friends after their "advice."

Whether believers realize it or not, their images of God influence *everything* they do: the way they pray in church, the words of comfort they offer in a hospital room, the simple but nitty-gritty acts of charity like offering to sit with a sick person for a few hours so a family member can take a much-needed rest. When we remember the needs of all God's people in common prayer, we can do that so as to thank God that we do not have those same needs or we can join in those prayers and become more compassionate, not

toward anonymous masses of people but to Jane, the grieving widow with two children under five, or to Ted, the
discouraged fifty-year-old seeking new employment. Jesus
said of the Pharisees that their words were bold but their
deeds were few (Mt 23:4). Common prayer can mask
Pharisaic hard-heartedness or can encourage bold deeds of
compassion.

Worshipers can also ask themselves if their common
prayer—and the acts of charity which should flow from
worship—really take notice of the suffering members. Or
is this worship only for people "who've got it all together"—like the men and women in Jesus' day who loved
the temple worship but would not have noticed the hungry,
the naked, etc.? It would be encouraging but dishonest to
report that such spiritual blindness has been completely
cured.

Works of Charity

Common prayer can help show a group's concern for
suffering men and women, but that prayer must encourage
concrete acts of charity. The Good Samaritan probably remembered the world's suffering people in his prayers, but
Jesus praises him for a very specific act of charity shown to
the man left half-dead on the road from Jerusalem to Jericho. Perhaps the priest and levite in that story thought,
"I'll pray for him." That's fine, of course, but the Good
Samaritan found a way to help the man *and* pray for him.
A spiritual work of mercy did not substitute for a corporal
work of mercy.

Toward the end of his apostolic letter on suffering,
Pope John Paul II says that the parable of the Good
Samaritan

witnesses to the fact that Christ's revelation of the sal-
vific meaning of suffering *is in no way identified with an
attitude of passivity* [Pope's emphasis]. Completely the
reverse is true. The Gospel is the negation of passivity
in the face of suffering. Christ himself is especially active in this field. (§30)

If Christians remain passive toward the sufferings of others,
they fail to live out the two great commandments and
thereby, in a sense, become "the devil's martyrs," encouraging belief in a cruel God.

What does a compassionate community look like?
More and more parishes and congregations have a ministry
to the grieving which helps not only at funerals but in the
weeks and months afterward. St. Vincent de Paul groups
and similar organizations offer people in need assistance
with basics such as food, shelter and clothing. A compassionate community works through groups organized around
a particular need and through individuals ready to respond
to a variety of needs. The compassionate community need
not be religiously-based. Bread for the World, for example,
counts men and women of diverse beliefs but agreed on the
need to fight world hunger. A compassionate community
can say "We're sorry" for past sufferings it may have
caused; thus it wants to repair the damage. In recent years,
for example, some parishes have invited former Catholics
to make their peace with the Church. Usually that has
meant listening to a lot of anger or resentment toward a
Church person who had caused the individual a great deal
of suffering. One Lent a group of Franciscans in Manhattan
took out newspaper ads inviting unchurched Catholics to
"Come home for Easter." Of the 521 people who wrote in
response to the ad or attended one of the follow-up meet-
ings, most had a painful memory of a Church experience;

few had fundamental faith problems. A compassionate community forgives and can ask for forgiveness.

The followers of Jesus show compassion by working to bind up individual wounds (as the Good Samaritan did), but they also work against *systemic* evil, the evil which has become so widely accepted that often people cannot imagine a world without it. For example, some Christians in the Roman Empire fought slavery not only by "buying" slaves and then freeing them but also by working to abolish the laws which made slavery legal. Today the fight against systemic evil is directed toward world hunger, the arms race and disrespect for life at all stages—to name only three examples among many.

Much as we admire people who may be famous for binding up individual wounds, we need to work against whatever systems may foster inhuman conditions and relationships. Pope Paul VI once said, "If you want peace, work for justice." Working for justice, of course, can be much more dangerous than individual acts of charity. The Catholic practice of honoring the saints represents one way of showing that the same person can address individual suffering and communal injustice. Other religious groups may not have saints in the Roman Catholic sense, but they have a sense of which men and women have lived out the two great commandments with extraordinary courage and exemplary self-sacrifice.

Holy men and women remind us of the solidarity between the living and those who already see God face to face. God did not abandon them in their time of need nor will he abandon us. Saintly women and men make the Gospel very concrete—in this time and place, amid these difficulties, showing God's compassion not to people in the abstract but to individuals who need life's basic necessities or encouragement for the human spirit. Saintly men and women choose life; in some way they all suffer and yet day after day they choose to respond with compassion instead of bitterness.

The saints prayed, asked pardon for their sins and failings and then lived out the good news. They have modeled not only good citizenship here and now but also a strong belief in God's kingdom not yet fully established. No one of them possessed all the gifts that Christ's body needs, but together they witness powerfully to the heavenly kingdom where God will be all anyone will need.

Bitterness or Compassion?

A compassionate community cannot make an individual's pain go away completely but it can try to alleviate that pain and then suffer alongside the person, offering ways to bear some of the pain and making sure that the suffering person feels very much a part of this community. Any group can do only so much. Large communities can never offer support in quite the way that good friends can.

To paraphrase the Flannery O'Connor quote used in the Introduction, the tragedy of many people is that they do not know what to do with their suffering. A community can either encourage the suffering person to take the road of compassion and greater solidarity or it can give that person even more reason to choose the road of bitterness and withdrawal. The community cannot make anyone's choice, of course, but it should try to live with a clear conscience.

The community can be a foretaste of the heavenly banquet where every tear will be wiped away, or it can weaken faith by ignoring the gap between generous words and less generous actions. The Christian community can help people deal with their anger at God, or it can encourage shame over having such feelings. It can pray honestly (ready to act in compassion) or fraudulently (excusing itself from compassion). But no community is some distant and anonymous "they"—it's you and I and millions of other women, men and children with individual talents, weaknesses, a sense of conscience and, like the Good Samaritan, a willingness to take the risks which compassion always requires.

For Personal Reflection

1. Have I ever felt pain like Job's and received only a self-serving theological answer? Why didn't I quit believing in God?

2. Who has given me time and space to express anger at God? How did that affect my relations with God?

3. Because of my unique history, could I be in a good position to help someone suffering a similar painful loss (death of a spouse, blindness, etc.)?

4. Has my joining in common prayer ever led me to an act of compassion I might otherwise not have done?

5. Have I experienced prayer being used as a substitute for an act of charity? Have I ever done that?

6. Do individuals and groups in my parish invite suffering people to group celebrations, or do we simply wonder why so-and-so doesn't come anymore?

For Group Discussion

1. Why do friendships either grow or shrink—but not remain the same—when someone is suffering?

2. Have we seen suffering women and men choose to respond in acts of charity?

3. Do you belong to any group sponsoring a support group, hotline or similar response to human suffering?

4. Have you ever seen common prayer leading to increased compassion? Did that compassion lead back into common prayer?

5. Have you ever seen Christians practicing a non-Gospel passivity in the face of evil?

6. How can a community help a person decide what to do with his/her suffering?

Resources

1. Arthur Miller, *The Death of a Salesman.*

2. James McNamara, *The Power of Compassion: Innocence and Powerlessness as Adversaries in the Spiritual Life* (Paulist, 1983).

3. Carol Luebering and Robert E. Schmitz, *Nothing To Fear: Unleashing the Power of the Resurrection* (St. Anthony Messenger, 1985).

4. Avery Dulles, S.J., *A Church To Believe In: Discipleship and the Dynamics of Freedom* (Crossroad, 1985).

5. Henri Nouwen, Donald McNeill, Douglas Morrison, *Compassion: A Reflection on the Christian Life* (Doubleday, 1983).

6. Viktor Frankl, *Man's Search for Meaning* (Washington Square Press/Simon and Schuster, 1985).

7. Jean Vanier, *Community and Growth: Our Pilgrimage Together* (Paulist, 1979)